# Teamwork 9.0

*Successful Workgroup Problem Solving
Using the Enneagram*

Matt Schlegel

ISBN: 978-1-7334788-2-3 (Print: *Teamwork 9.0* — Color)
ISBN: 978-1-7334788-0-9 (Print: *Teamwork 9.0* — B&W)
ISBN: 978-1-7334788-1-6 (E-book)

Library of Congress Control Number: 2019913218

Cover layout, interior design/layout, and proofreading by Joanne Shwed, Backspace Ink (backspaceink.com)

Cover design and cover content consulting by JMF and SR (PerfectAsAlways.com)

Editing by DeAnna Burghart

Illustrations by James Yamasaki (JamesYamasaki.com)

# Praise for *Teamwork 9.0*

"*Teamwork 9.0* is like a 'secret decoder ring' that will help you understand other people and work with them far more effectively. If only I'd had this when I first started working!"

Kimberly Wiefling—Leadership consultant and
author of *Scrappy Project Management*

"*Teamwork 9.0* is a must read for all new and experienced team leaders. Matt Schlegel's practical approach and easy-to-understand examples demystify the complexities of the Enneagram and help you recognize the value that each of your team members brings to problem solving and the innovation process. He introduces a series of tools that can be adapted to many different working environments. I wish I had had this book earlier in my career."

Susan Schwartz—Management consultant and
author of *Creating a Greater Whole: A Project
Manager's Guide to Becoming a Leader*

"Remember that team you were on where things just worked? Everyone contributed and it seemed there was no challenge the team couldn't solve. Remember those other teams that got stuck, people didn't pull their weight, and just didn't ever seem to click? Read *Teamwork 9.0* and learn how to make all your teams like the first. You might even learn something about yourself in the process."

Scot Kleinman—Associate Director,
Development at Gemini Observatory

"If you manage high-throughput teams where collaboration is a requirement and not a luxury, you MUST read *Teamwork 9.0*. Matt Schlegel is a master at identifying behavioral characteristics that can be shaped and nurtured to create functional and effective teams, even if those behavioral characteristics run the gamut. I am speaking from experience. Matt provided an Enneagram workshop to my team of 18 almost two years ago and a week doesn't go by without one of them citing the principles Matt taught them, and now lays out in this book in an easy-to-read-and-implement manner. You have nothing to lose and everything to gain by following Matt's pithy but perceptive road map to building more effective and collaborative teams."

Neil J. Beaton—Managing Director,
Alvarez & Marsal Valuation Services

"If you are interested in understanding team construction and dynamics and collaborative problem solving, you should read *Teamwork 9.0*. It is intricate and rich while very practical. Matt Schlegel frames a comprehensive methodology that explains how to match people to tasks, situations and, most importantly, other people. The tools he presents make these challenges easy to address quickly, efficiently, and effectively."

Gideon Shaanan—Founder, Osenti

"As a leadership educator and coach, I've been looking for a way to bring the value of the Enneagram to executives and teams, and *Teamwork 9.0* is the answer. Very readable and relatable; the insights and strategies that Matt Schlegel provides will solve many of the elusive mysteries behind successful collaboration."

Lucy Freedman—Coauthor, *Smart Work: The SYNTAX Guide to Influence* and founder/CEO of Syntax for Change

"*Teamwork 9.0* took me on a practical and entertaining journey that allowed me, and will allow you, to use the Enneagram in business and personal situations. Whatever your type is, you will get practical advice on how to develop your skills and gain a strategic advantage. Whether you are a leader or a teammate who wants to participate on highly effective teams, there is plenty of information here to help you develop your skills for connecting and working with people."

Adrian Bray—Co-CEO and founder, AssayCS Inc.

"As a continuous student of leadership, culture, and team performance, I found that *Teamwork 9.0* really answered many of my unresolved questions. Matt Schlegel has done an excellent job sharing how the Enneagram is an amazing system to maximize team effectiveness."

Frumi Rachel Barr, MBA, PhD—Leadership consultant and
author of *A CEO's Secret Weapon: How to Accelerate Success*

"Read this book to get a better understanding of how people react to different situations based on their personality traits. This is very helpful information in trying to understand group dynamics."

Pat Grogan—Sr. VP of Operations, NewTek

"If you are an organizational development person and an Enneagram fan read *Teamwork 9.0* immediately. The Enneagram is an insightful tool into human differences and patterns of growth and change. Using an analytical model that takes successful human relationships beyond the realm of mystery is a gift for anyone challenged to understand what works and what doesn't when it comes to the dynamics of collaboration and team building. Matt Schlegel has made a valuable contribution to the field. Applying his thinking and analysis will go a long way in helping you to both understand and choose behaviors that contribute to powerful collaborations."

Stewart Levine—Management consultant and author of *Getting to Resolution* and *The Book of Agreement and Collaboration 2.0*

"Matt Schlegel brings the Enneagram alive! It becomes more than a theory but an energy that we can feel in ourselves and others."

Rev. Roger Morimoto—Pastor, Aldersgate United
Methodist Church, Palo Alto, Calif.

"We learn about personality dynamics of team participants while *Teamwork 9.0* successfully explains how leaders and managers can elicit better performance in the professional sandbox. A must read!"

Stevie Bobes—Founder, Wine Ambassadeur

"*Teamwork 9.0* helps managers unlock the hidden potential buried within their organizations. For those who have been perplexed why certain groups fail, underperform, or just don't jell well, the book gives you the framework for building supercharged teams."

Marc Bookman—Founder and CEO, Opu Labs,
Arigo Entertainment, TrendLife, Sentius

"Matt Schlegel superbly identifies and explains the personality differences that dictate how team members relate to, and communicate with, each other. Read *Teamwork 9.0* to unlock the secrets of improving team creativity, energy, and productivity."

Stephen L. Dobrow—CEO, Primark Benefits

# Contents

# List of Tables and Figures

# Foreword

This book provides profound insights into the optimal management of employees in a business. But, in my opinion, these insights reach much further, offering exciting explanations of the very foundation of human society.

To explain this bold opinion, I'll begin with my own experience with the Enneagram theory, which began in the early 1990s. Back then, I was in a soon-to-be-failed first marriage. Some friends recommended an Enneagram book, which I read with tepid interest before moving on to other topics.

By the late 1990s, I was recently divorced and pondering human nature. These same friends rerecommended the same Enneagram book. But this time when I read it, the pages seemed to scream Truth. In particular, the pithy explanation of the relationship dynamic between a person of my type and that of my ex-wife caught my attention. It was an eerily accurate description of a twelve-year relationship. I read every other combination of relationships described in that book and none of the others came close. Only these two pages that dispassionately laid out a road map for those twelve years did the job.

"How could that be?" I asked myself. How could an author who had never met me or my ex-wife accurately describe the dynamics of our relationship?

It was the search for answers to these open questions that drove me deep into the neuroscience of emotions in the early 2000s. I was looking for brain studies that spoke to the same emotional states described in the Enneagram theory.

Pondering these studies, I came upon a hypothesis suggesting a correlation between the Enneagram and certain patterns of asymmetric activation in two sets of bilateral brain sites (amygdala and prefrontal cortex). As of this writing, this hypothesis is neither proven nor debunked. It remains open.

Matt writes about this hypothesis [see "Work Team Triads" on page 209]. In the mid-2000s, I self-published this theory of mine, hoping to interest someone in these arcane ideas. Not long afterward, Matt reached out to me, and ten years after our first meeting our collaboration on all matters Enneagram continues.

So when Matt began writing this book, I was one of the people he asked to review it. As I read this book for the first time, my jaw kept dropping until it finally hit the floor around Chapter 5, where he discusses the relationship between Enneagram types and creativity [see Chapter 5, "The Creativity Seesaw," on page 139].

Let me share one aspect of my astonishment. My hypothesis, if true, says that the Enneagram can be described as certain patterns of activation in the brain. It says nothing about why those patterns emerged in the first place.

That is what the chapter on problem solving [see Chapter 2, "Problem Solving with the Enneagram," on page 63] is for. I know that chapter describes an approach for solving vexing problems within a company. Certainly, Matt does a splendid job articulating this.

But I think this problem-solving approach of Matt's goes way beyond business—into human society itself. Why did humans, millions of years ago, band into social tribes and clans rather than go through life as more or less singletons, as do some species?

I suggest that the answer starts with observing that the core reason for banding with other people is to solve problems (starvation, violence, early mortality, etc.) rather than merely to share the spoils of a charmed life.

What is the best group of people for solving a problem? Should they all think and feel and react in the same way? Team sports teach us early on that this would be a foolish way to populate a team. When all or most of the team members are carbon copies of each other, that team tends to lose, no matter how individually talented the members are. In contrast, teams with a diverse set of personalities, with different optimal roles assigned to each, tend to win (talent being at least close).

I suspect that early on, nature selected for diverse clans of people that assigned the proper roles to the clan members. Now I realize that the theory of natural selection concerns individuals, not clans. But maybe, just maybe, Matt's book is the gateway to understanding optimal adaptation at the group level.

And if that's too lofty a goal for this book, rest assured that Matt presents a road map for optimal team collaboration. In other words, this book lays out for you the path to success in your business.

Peter Savich
Author, *Personality and the Brain*

# Preface

I worked for a brilliant scientist who reenvisioned how electronic displays convey information. She had studied visual processing in humans and understood that conventional RGB stripe displays were grossly inefficient. Theoretically, she could convey in five pixels the same information conveyed by twelve RGB stripe pixels. I was fortunate to be a part of the team developing new technology based on this insight. Once our imaginations were released from the constraints of conventional pixel layouts, we found ourselves tripping over novel ideas for better, more efficient displays. Those ideas are now incorporated into many of today's smartphone displays.

At about this same time, I was introduced to the Enneagram and had a similar experience of wide-open exploration and discovery with it. Ever a student of ways to facilitate better cooperation and productivity among teams, I was fascinated with the elements of the Enneagram system. As I became more familiar with it, I discovered innovative ways to apply the Enneagram to work teams. I want to share these innovative methods with work team leaders interested in improving team effectiveness.

My goal with this book is to demonstrate a practical application of the Enneagram using tools applicable to the workplace. While some Enneagram practitioners explore spiritual aspects of the system, that is not my focus or intent here. I do not begrudge that point of view, but my take of the Enneagram tends to be on the pragmatic side. I want to deliver the best possible tools to help teams of people work together effectively to accomplish their mission. What I hope you will take from this book is that using the Enneagram only as a personality typing system just scratches the surface of the power that the Enneagram system offers. In this book, I will share with you how the Enneagram can also be used to help you and your teams work together to solve the problems you need to solve.

## *Work Team Leaders*

This book is for work team leaders—business owners and executives, group managers, project managers, etc.—who want to understand how their teams can perform better. The Enneagram provides a framework and a vocabulary for discussing team dynamics and the issues that arise as teams work together to address challenges and solve problems. Through the lens of the Enneagram, I will provide new perspectives on the issues that keep teams from working together well and show how team leaders can guide teams to overcome challenges and keep moving forward.

A working understanding of the Enneagram is required to get the most out of the ideas in this book. Chapter 1, "The Enneagram Briefly," on page 31 provides a brief overview of the Enneagram, but this is by no means a thorough treatment of the subject. *The Enneagram Made Easy* by Renee Baron and Elizabeth Wagele provides a terrific introduction to the system.

The words used to describe the nine Enneagram types vary from author to author. Chapter 1 develops the vocabulary used throughout the rest of this book. As an aside, this book substitutes the gender-neutral *they* and *their* for gender-specific pronouns when speaking in general terms.

The heart of this book starts at Chapter 2, "Problem Solving with the Enneagram," on page 63 where I introduce the Enneagram as a framework that describes how humans solve problems—both as individuals and, more powerfully, as work teams.

## Enneagram and Work Teams: The Journey

The chapters of this book are in roughly the same order as my journey of discovery. After studying the Enneagram for some time, I started to ponder why Enneagram Type 1 was labeled 1, why Type 2 was labeled 2, and so on. Why not label the types with letters? Or colors? Or animals? Or planets? When I posed this question to one of my Enneagram mentors, he suggested I read *The Secret of Enneagrams: Mapping the Personality* by Klausbernd Vollmar.

In his book, Vollmar shows how the Enneagram can be used not only to describe personality types but to describe processes in nature as well. The Enneagram numbers represent both the dynamics related to each step in the process and the sequential order of those dynamics. Reflecting on this, I imagined how the Enneagram could be used to describe the process by which people work together to solve problems.

As a result of this reflection, I developed a unique problem-solving process based on the Enneagram, which I describe in Chapter 2. The sequence of this process lines up exactly with the order of the Enneagram types (numbers). I started applying this process with my coworkers, and the results were dramatically successful. I applied the methodology on multiple initiatives with separate teams, and it proved reliable and robust, leading to successful and persistent outcomes. These results inspired and motivated me to write this book and share my experiences.

As I exercised the Enneagram-based problem-solving methodology with work teams, I noticed the natural emergence of *shared leadership*: each phase of problem solving requires a unique set of skills, and team members naturally possessing those skills emerge as leaders during the related phase.

Chapter 3, "Shared Leadership," on page 97 describes shared leadership and the unique contributions of each Enneagram type during problem solving. Passing the leadership baton from step to step allows the team to tap into the best attributes of all team members at the optimal time. Sharing leadership creates a sense of ownership and enthusiasm in both the process and the results. The team builds and maintains the momentum necessary to achieve the goal and solve the problem.

Chapter 4, "The Leadership Path of Growth," on page 121 answers the question of how to accomplish more with fewer people by using the Enneagram's concept of the path of integration. An ideal problem-solving team would have at least one of each of the nine Enneagram types. Since most will not, team members need a way to access the dynamics of the missing types. The Enneagram's path of integration opens the door to that access.

The *path of integration* is the calm, secure state of each Enneagram type. In that state, each type can access the dynamic of any other Enneagram type, enabling each person to more fully contribute to the success of the team. Creating a work environment that allows team members to operate in their secure state helps them move along their path of integration where they will have access to all the dynamics necessary for successful problem solving. By accessing the talents of the other Enneagram types, your teams can solve problems with fewer team members.

Chapter 5, "The Creativity Seesaw," on page 139 shows how creativity emerges from each Enneagram type. I introduce the concept of the Creativity Seesaw and show how the creative engine of each type can be described by seesaw transitions between the path of integration and the path of disintegration, giving each Enneagram type a distinct creative energy. Creativity is essential to successful problem solving and is required at each step in the process. Each Enneagram type can contribute their distinct creative talents, and this chapter elaborates on how each type can access those talents.

Working with teams over the years, I have noticed that not only do team members demonstrate specific strengths associated with their Enneagram type, each type relates to time differently. As I show in Chapter 6, "The Enneagram and Time," on page 165, there are two unique aspects of time to consider. The first is that each Enneagram type directs most of their mental energy towards a specific point on a timeline. For instance, Type 6 tends to spend mental energy imagining various scenarios in the future, while Type 2 tends to reflect on relationships and experiences in the past. I will share my observations of where along the timeline each Enneagram type devotes their mental energy and the importance of these various perspectives to collective problem solving.

The second aspect of time I have noticed is whether or not time itself is a motivating force for each Enneagram type. For instance, when presented with a deadline, some Enneagram types feel an innate sense of urgency to meet that deadline, while others feel no such compulsion. In other words, Enneagram types with a strong sense of patience will not be motivated by the simple passing of minutes on a clock, while those with a strong sense of urgency will be compelled to action. The interplay between a sense of urgency and a sense of patience is another key ingredient to successful team collaboration and problem solving, which we will examine in Chapter 6.

Chapter 7, "Work Team Triads: Two Balanced Brains," on page 201 theorizes a connection between the Enneagram and the brain. Having a science and engineering background and being by nature a skeptical type (yes, I am an Enneagram Type 6), I am compelled to continually test the Enneagram framework. After working with the Enneagram for several years and discovering how robustly it stands up to my scrutiny, it occurred to me that, to have such a wide range of applicability to human behavior and interactions, there must be some physiological basis for the Enneagram.

Intent on investigating this connection, I stumbled across *Personality and the Brain* by Peter Savich (see the WebBook at personalityandthebrain.org/WebBook/Introduction.htm). Savich maps out how dominances in certain parts of the brain—specifically the amygdala and the prefrontal cortex—appear to line up neatly with the nine dynamics of the Enneagram. Having tied brain function to behavior, I surmised that the Enneagram provides a framework for understanding how humans evolved to cooperate with each other and how each of us contributes specific talents to problem solving.

In many workplaces I have noticed that certain Enneagram types tend to coalesce naturally into work teams. I use Savich's theory to explain why this happens. I share these observations in Chapter 7 and introduce the concept of *work team triads*—the teams that naturally work well together because of their balance of brain dominances.

I devote Chapter 8, "Team Diagnostics Toolbox," on page 227 to describing tools I have developed based on all these concepts. I explain how team leaders can analyze their teams, understand strengths and weaknesses, and prescribe solutions to help their teams work together successfully. The tools are meant to illustrate adjustments team leaders can make to address the challenges unique to specific team composition. Since the possible combinations of Enneagram types on a team are practically endless, the tools can reduce the numerous possibilities into understandable categories that make the job of addressing the variations much more manageable. Using these tools, team leaders can understand the dynamics that can either slow down the team or accelerate their progress towards a goal.

Finally, in Chapter 9, "The Meaning of Life," on page 257, I reflect on the purpose of the Enneagram and of each of the nine dynamics. I am excited to have this opportunity to share with you the insights I have gleaned using the Enneagram and the tools I have developed to help teams work together more effectively. Whatever the scope and scale of the problem you are tackling—project, organizational, community, national, or global—I believe that the tools presented here will help you move your team forward as fast as humanly possible. I hope you will experience delight and success on your problem-solving journey.

# Acknowledgments

Problem solving using the Enneagram as a framework generates a powerful and exciting response from teams. After enjoying facilitating the process for seven years, I wanted to find a way to share these methods broadly. I attended a workshop led by my dear friend, colleague, and mentor Kimberly Wiefling during which I envisioned writing a book on the subject. That was 2010. Now, ten years later, I am proud, pleased, and relieved to present this work. My deepest appreciation to Kimberly for the vision and encouragement over the years. Thank you, Kimberly!

My journey with the Enneagram started and continues to this day under the enthusiastic tutelage of Rev. Roger Morimoto. I am grateful for all his support over the years. He provides many of the wonderful anecdotes that appear here. And he has created a learning environment at the Center for Spiritual Life (CSL) in Palo Alto where a group of Enneagram enthusiasts share experiences and learn from one another. Thank you, Roger and all CSL participants!

Had I not discovered Peter Savich's theory that ties the Enneagram to the brain, I might never have fully developed my thinking on these topics. In this book, I share Peter's theory and extend its application to team effectiveness and team composition. This is a case of standing on the shoulders of a giant, especially since Peter is a former professional basketball player! Peter's exuberant support of my work provides me with endless motivation. Thank you, Peter!

I wanted to share my book creation journey with a coach and put to the test my theory on selecting coaches. Lucy Freedman was an obvious choice for me. Not only does she lie on my Enneagram path of integration as a Type 9, she published a book on workplace effectiveness: *Smart Work: The SYNTAX Guide to Influence.* Lucy has been a steady guide on my journey, keeping me focused on the big objectives and diving into the details when necessary. I couldn't have asked for a better coach. Thank you, Lucy!

What better way to bring the book to life than with stories, and what better way to convey those stories than with the brilliant illustrations of Jimmy Yamasaki. Jimmy understands exactly what I want to communicate and finds a fun and thought-provoking illustration that makes the point. Jimmy has accompanied me on my book journey from the beginning, and I am so grateful for his friendship and contributions. Thank you, Jimmy!

I deliberately solicited feedback from all Enneagram types as I developed my manuscript. I wanted each type's perspective on the work, and their feedback informed the writing. My sincerest thanks go out to Stevie Bobes, Scot Kleinman, Stephen Dobrow, Chris Thollaug, Gideon Shaanan, Marc Bookman, Stewart Levine, Adrian Bray, Judy Thompson, Laura and Jeffry Fulp, and Jill and Neil Beaton.

I was so happy when editor DeAnna Burghart self-identified as Enneagram Type 1. My intention was to hire a 1 for the job, and I was elated that DeAnna was not only a 1 but an Enneagram-aware 1. My good luck! Not only did DeAnna perfect my prose, she did so with both grace and humor that made what would have otherwise been an arduous job a chuckle-filled delight. Thank you, DeAnna!

Thanks to my mom Robin Schlegel for feedback and proofreading of my earliest manuscripts—writing only a mother could love. I appreciate her patience and support for this project and for all my endeavors. Thank you, Mom!

ACKNOWLEDGMENTS

Thanks to my extended family, without a doubt my most informative instructors on human nature. Each has given me insight into their specific Enneagram types. Many of the insights I describe here have come from those interactions as we have lived our lives together in unguarded expressions of ourselves. And special thanks to my wonderful wife Helen and kids Sakura, Kiki, and Nicholas. I am proud of them as they fulfill being their best possible selves.

# CHAPTER 1

# The Enneagram Briefly

Once you understand the Enneagram you start to see it everywhere. I see it especially in films and TV shows where a type's characteristics are often exaggerated and portrayed in a dramatic or humorous fashion. Family is also a terrific venue for exploring Enneagram types; I am fortunate enough that within my close family all nine Enneagram types are represented.

By the time I started studying the Enneagram, many of my family members were already up to speed. When I told my family that I tested highly for Type 8, the Type 8 in the family declared that I was actually Type 6. I learned then that Type 8s are very direct. I also learned that Enneagram questionnaires are better at telling us what we are not than what we are.

The Enneagram is commonly used as a personality typing system, and it is effective in that application. There is a broad range of behaviors associated with each type, and the Enneagram explains these variations well. The system also explains how the behaviors of each type can vary based on our state of security or insecurity. As a family, we had a great deal of fun using the system to better understand ourselves and our interpersonal interactions.

My initial exposure to the Enneagram left me even more curious. Are we born with our Enneagram type, or does it emerge based on our experiences (nature versus nurture)? As opposed to other widely used personality typing systems, why are there nine types and not sixteen as in Myers-Briggs or four as in DISC? (Both Myers-Briggs and DISC are behavioral assessment tools.) Is the number assignment arbitrary or is there a reason for the specific sequence? Can I be any type if I choose? And why can't I be a 10?

I am joking about the last question, though I hear it all the time. But these questions motivated my deeper exploration of the Enneagram. In this chapter, I provide a brief overview of the Enneagram system and set the table for using the Enneagram as a tool for team-based problem solving.

The purpose of this chapter is threefold: 1) to serve as a compact refresher for those already familiar with the Enneagram; 2) to highlight the characteristics of each type that are important to team collaboration and team-based problem solving (discussed in later chapters); and 3) to serve as a handy reference of the nine Enneagram types as you work your way through the book.

In my descriptions of the Enneagram types, I will sometimes refer to the *energy* of a particular type. I treat systems, organic or inorganic, as flows of energy. Much as our bodies require energy—food—to animate us, each Enneagram type serves as a distinct energy for our interpersonal interactions. I use the word *dynamic* in the same vein as I use the word *energy*.

## The Enneagram Diagram

First, let's examine the diagram that is commonly used to represent the Enneagram (derived from the Greek word *ennea*, nine).

The diagram has nine points, which can be divided into three *triads* with three points each. The triads (8-9-1), (2-3-4), and (5-6-7) are called the main triads of the Enneagram and, as such, are often referred to as *centers*. Though there are several words commonly used to describe each of these centers, I have chosen to use descriptive phrases: Types 8, 9, and 1 comprise the Gut-Intuitive-Anger center; Types 2, 3, and 4 are the Heart-Feeling-Emotion center; and Types 5, 6, and 7 are the Head-Thinking-Anxiety center.

## *The Wizard of Oz*

The Enneagram centers remind me of *The Wizard of Oz*. On her journey, Dorothy encounters three companions—the Lion, the Tin Man, and the Scarecrow. Each of these companions represents an archetype described by the Enneagram centers: the Lion who wants courage represents the Gut-Intuitive-Anger center; the Tin Man who wants a heart represents the Heart-Feeling-Emotion center; and the Scarecrow who wants a brain represents the Head-Thinking-Anxiety center.

My descriptive phrases for the Enneagram centers start with a body part, followed by a function often ascribed to that body part, and finally a word used to describe a reaction to a threat. For instance, the Gut types are often thought of as being most in tune with their intuition, their gut reaction. When people of the Gut-Intuitive-Anger center are threatened, anger drives their response. These three words distinctively describe this center: Gut-Intuitive-Anger. Likewise for the Heart-Feeling-Emotion center and the Head-Thinking-Anxiety center.

The most revealing behaviors for each Enneagram type occur when that type is reacting to a threat or is under stress. Thus, it is easier to identify someone's Enneagram type when they are under pressure. Naturally, the behaviors people exhibit when threatened are not the most flattering. A discussion of stress responses can be off-putting to many people. Please bear with me during this section and understand that I highlight both positive and negative behaviors to help you more easily distinguish and identify the nine different types.

Let's briefly examine the three types that comprise each center. Referring to Table 1.1, each center has a primary stress response (anger, emotion, and anxiety), and that response can take one of three forms: an external expression, an internal expression, or a suppressed expression. It is important to understand the concept of external, internal, and suppressed expressions, so the descriptions that follow Table 1.1 are in that order, even though it seems "out of order" numerically. The goal of these descriptions is for you to appreciate the motivations, responses, and characteristics of each type.

### Table 1.1 – Summary of the Nine Enneagram Types

| Type | Label* | Primary Response |
|:---:|:---:|:---:|
| **Gut-Intuitive-Anger Center** | | |
| 8 | The Asserter | External Anger |
| 9 | The Peacemaker | Suppressed Anger |
| 1 | The Perfectionist | Internal Anger |
| **Heart-Feeling-Emotion Center** | | |
| 2 | The Helper | External Emotion |
| 3 | The Achiever | Suppressed Emotion |
| 4 | The Romantic | Internal Emotion |
| **Head-Thinking-Anxiety Center** | | |
| 7 | The Adventurer | External Anxiety |
| 6 | The Questioner | Suppressed Anxiety |
| 5 | The Observer | Internal Anxiety |

*These are the labels used by Baron and Wagele in *The Enneagram Made Easy*, which I have adopted for this book.

# The Gut-Intuitive-Anger Center

First, let's look at Types 8, 1, and 9 in the Gut-Intuitive-Anger center. The types in this triad respond with anger when under stress or threat: Type 8 responds with the external expression of anger; Type 1, the internal expression; and Type 9, the suppressed expression.

### Type 8 – The Asserter
### "Getting to Action"

As the external anger type, the 8 is the most comfortable of all the types at expressing outward-directed anger. This is their natural response to stress, and it's an effective tool for them to achieve their ends. The 8s are concerned with maintaining control of their environment. When that control is threatened, the anger response emerges. They rarely back down from a challenge or confrontation. As such, the 8 is frequently called the Asserter. Often, 8s are unaware that they are displaying anger, even while those around them recoil in surprise, shock, or horror. After their anger subsides, Type 8s can go about their business as if nothing happened, while others around the 8 may still harbor residual feelings of anxiety, hurt, or resentment.

In the workplace, 8s tend to migrate towards action-oriented leadership roles. They tend to be very confident people. Being in the intuitive center, Type 8s are guided by a strong sense of intuition. This can frustrate data-driven people (those in the thinking center) or emotion-driven people (those in the feeling center). The 8s are eager to jump into action based on their gut instincts. Whereas other types value discussion, the impatient 8 typically prefers to skip the debate and begin the task. Type 8s embody a combination of assertiveness, instincts, and action that serves them well in leadership roles.

## Type 1 – The Perfectionist
## "Identifying Problems"

Next, we turn to the internal anger type, Type 1. Instead of directing the anger response outward like the 8, the natural response of Type 1s directs anger inward, towards themselves. Type 1s will describe a critical voice inside their head, pointing out that something is not right and that they could do more to correct it. Because this internal critic motivates the 1 to work hard until things are perfect, Type 1 is often called the Perfectionist.

Although Type 1s are highly motivated by their internal critic, they intensely dislike criticism from others. Generally, they have already criticized themselves extensively, so the external critic only reminds the 1s that whatever they are working on is not yet perfect or can never be perfect. The inability to achieve perfection causes the 1 to feel frustrated—a common feeling for them.

In the workplace, if a task needs precision, the 1s are usually the perfect people to do it. You just have to allow them ample time, since getting it done right is more important to them than getting it done on time. Also, if you need a comprehensive understanding of any problem, the 1 is the person to pick it apart and know it inside and out. Type 1s excel at identifying and investigating problems; they are highly tuned for the job of root cause analysis or wherever precision is required.

## Type 9 – The Peacemaker
## "Seeking Harmony"

Positioned between Types 8 and 1 in the Gut-Intuitive-Anger center, Type 9 is the *core type* of this triad and represents the *suppressed* reaction—in this case, suppressed anger. Imagine having so much anger inside you—though there may not be any conscious awareness of it—that the only way to negotiate the world is to suppress that anger. Type 9s are so sensitive to anger that the moment they wake in the morning, they are thinking about how to address the needs and wants of others in order to minimize disagreements. That constant pursuit of eliminating conflict gives 9s the Peacemaker label.

Curiously, Type 9s are so focused on others' desires that they have trouble conveying their own needs and wants, even when asked directly. They may opt to say what they think others want to hear, and in doing so avoid any possibility of conflict. Another conflict avoidance strategy of the 9 is sleep; there is no conflict with others when you are sleeping, so Type 9s love to sleep.

In the workplace, 9s tend to assume roles in which their peacemaking skills are highly valued. For instance, peacemaking skills are important to the role of project manager. Even if they aren't 9s, people in project manager roles will have to behave like 9s much of the time. Also, 9s are great at customer service. There is no better type to calm an agitated customer and to help them address their issue. The 9 seeks harmony in the environment and is compelled to achieve it.

# The Heart-Feeling-Emotion Center

Next, we move on to the Heart-Feeling-Emotion center. Again, there is an external response type, an internal response type, and a suppressed response type. People in the Heart-Feeling-Emotion center are compelled to engage and interact with others—far more so than people in the other two centers, since the emotional interaction inherent to this center requires that there be someone to interact with. Let's take each expression in turn—external, internal, and suppressed.

## Type 2 – The Helper
## "Helping Others"

Type 2 is the external emotion response. The 2s strive to build an emotional connection with those around them, mainly by offering help. In return, Type 2s receive appreciation, which confirms they have established the emotional connection they crave.

For Type 2s, appreciation is like oxygen. Without constant appreciation they feel like they are suffocating. The fear of being unneeded—or worse, unwanted—drives the 2 to constantly help those around them. Because of this drive to help, 2s establish strong emotional connections with those in their lives. They have an innate sense of what others need and are driven to provide it.

The label often used to describe the 2 is the Helper. I frequently see 2s take on supporting roles in organizations—roles in which they can continuously interact with others, determine how they can help, and receive appreciation for that help. I also often see 2s in sales roles in which they understand customer needs and deliver solutions that meet those needs. Type 2s excel in roles that allow them to constantly interact with others, deliver assistance, and thereby receive appreciation.

## Type 4 – The Romantic
## "Feeling Everything"

Type 4 is the internal emotion response. If you ask 4s, "How are you feeling?" they may look at you somewhat mystified, not knowing how to answer. The 4s are feeling everything, so how can they pick just one feeling to share with you? If asked that question, 4s typically evade and don't share their true feelings; it is too difficult to explain, and they feel that you probably wouldn't understand anyway.

The 4s' sensitivity to feelings allows them to put themselves in others' emotional shoes. They have a sense for how people will react to a sunset, a painting, a poem, a song, an idea—they can detect the emotional content in almost anything and understand innately how other people will feel.

The description used for Type 4 is the Romantic. Type 4s often take on roles in art, music, writing, cuisine, product design, and marketing. These roles all deliver an emotional impact, leaving an impression on the recipient. The 4s get the most satisfaction when they have delivered that impression in a way that leaves the recipient at a loss for words to describe how they feel. When the 4s have accomplished that, they know that the recipient just got a taste of their world.

## Type 3 – The Achiever
## "Inspiration and Perspiration"

That brings us to Type 3, the core type for the Heart-Feeling-Emotion center—the suppressed emotion response. Imagine being so emotional that the only way to engage with the world is to suppress your emotions, whether or not you are conscious of them. As such, the 3 comes across as emotionally cool. And unlike 2s, who seek appreciation for their help, the 3s seek recognition for their achievements and successes. Having suppressed their own feelings, they seek external measures of their worth. Plus, directing others to focus on the 3's external accomplishments keeps the focus off their internal feelings.

Type 3 is called the Achiever. The 3s have incredible energy and willpower, which they apply to realizing successful outcomes. Because they suppress their feelings, they have difficulty conveying how they feel. This trait can leave coworkers confused about how the 3 feels about them, even when the 3 thinks highly of their colleagues!

When Type 3s are trying to get something done, it is easy for them to overlook the feelings of others. To someone who suppresses their feelings, a hammer, a screwdriver, a saw, a colleague, and a subordinate are all emotionally neutral tools. When the 3 starts to treat people like tools, conflict can arise. The 3s will plead that they are simply trying to get the job done in the most efficient way—which is true. What the 3s overlook, and are perhaps incapable of realizing, is how others are reacting to them and to their drive to get things done.

In addition to their amazing drive to succeed, 3s have the special ability to generate out-of-the-box ideas. For most of us, emotion, anxiety, or anger influence and restrict our ideas, but Type 3s do not filter ideas that way. Lacking these filters enables the 3 to freely throw out ideas to see how others react—like throwing spaghetti against a wall to see what sticks. The 3s are acutely aware of how others react to their ideas and will use those reactions to gauge which ideas are likely to be accepted. With a promising idea identified, the 3s can then direct their tremendous energy to bringing the idea to fruition. They are the true embodiment of both inspiration and perspiration.

This attention to how others react makes 3s ideal marketers and promoters. Their drive to succeed inspires others and serves them well in leadership roles. And their boundless energy keeps them and others on track to meet goals.

# The Head-Thinking-Anxiety Center

Next, we discuss the Head-Thinking-Anxiety center, in which anxiety is the primary response to stress. The main consideration for this triad is safety. When these types think that they are unsafe, anxiety arises. They are motivated to restore safety, thereby reducing anxiety—each with a different strategy.

### Type 7 – The Adventurer
### "Promoting a Plan for Fun"

Type 7 is the external anxiety response. The 7s are motivated to keep the mood and environment light and fun. They do not feel safe unless they think they are on good terms with everyone. When everyone is having a good time around them, the 7 feels safe and their anxiety level goes down.

Type 7 is called the Adventurer since they are always thinking about that next fun thing to do with everyone. In a social setting, the 7s especially want to know how they stand with each individual in the environment. They can tell this by receiving a warm greeting, a smile, a friendly handshake, a pat on the back, etc. As long as the relationship is on friendly terms, their anxiety level decreases.

The 7s' desire to know where they stand with others motivates them to interact with everyone around them. They are masters at networking or "working a room." Their compulsion to interact with people drives them into roles such as sales, marketing, and support.

Type 7s often try careers in politics. They are tireless networkers, seeking to get people excited about trying new things. They are always looking for something new to do, but they won't do it unless everyone else is on board. The 7s' gift is their ability to get everyone on board.

Their ability to promote ideas serves them well on teams and in leadership roles, whether in the political world or a company.

## Type 5 – The Observer
## "Analyzing Everything"

Type 5s have the internal anxiety response to stress. One of the drivers of that anxiety is the fear of being considered foolish. This fear drives the 5 to study, investigate, observe, and analyze everything that they think is important. Type 5s are also concerned with safety. They feel unsafe when they think that their resources may be depleted, so they are constantly seeking to collect and replenish resources—food, money, or anything else that makes them feel safe. For the 5, collecting resources, including information, is a primary source of safety.

Type 5s tend to be on the quiet side as they actively collect information from their environment, giving them the label of the Observer. If 5s equate information with a valuable resource like gold, then do you think that they are likely to part with it readily? Not a chance. The quiet 5s are reluctant communicators and only impart information if: 1) they share just enough content to make the person go away; or 2) they feel completely safe and confident and have no fear of being considered foolish.

Type 5s tend to be great at both collecting and analyzing data, and they often perform roles where they can focus on data rather than people. Type 5s are drawn to information-intensive roles, including academic, scientific, engineering, and financial roles. They are masters at picking apart data, analyzing it, and considering all possibilities. They are the ones who want to examine the entire menu. While they may be seeking the best option, there are often too many choices, which make it difficult for them to make a decision. For help with decision making, the 5s can turn to Type 6.

## Type 6 – The Questioner
## "Mapping the Future"

Type 6 is the suppressed anxiety response. Imagine having so much anxiety that the only way to engage with the world is to suppress it. Type 6 is the type that most often indicates that they feel a gnawing pit in their stomach. That pit is a symptom of their suppressed anxiety.

One way the 6s minimize their anxiety is by trying to understand the future. If they know what is going to happen, then their anxiety is diminished. In order to figure out what is going to happen, the 6 has to ask a lot of questions. It is this behavior that gives the 6 the label of the Questioner.

Because of their compulsion to reduce anxiety by understanding the future, the 6s are highly tuned to planning, budgeting, and setting up systems that deliver predictable outcomes. As long as the environment is calm and the future predictable, 6s can keep their anxiety at manageable levels. However, when life becomes less predictable and more chaotic, anxiety levels for the 6 will rise.

Because of their propensity to plan, Type 6s often migrate towards project management and accounting roles where they can track things important to them: people, time, and money. They naturally tend to perform worst-case analyses on plans, thereby helping a project or team avoid pitfalls. The 6s are typically not satisfied with a plan until they can visualize a clear path to the final goal. This ability to "see" the future serves them and their work teams well.

# Do You Recognize Anyone?

Did any of these descriptions match people you know? Some people more obviously express their Enneagram type than others. Were you able to identify yourself in any of these types? Often we can see ourselves in several types. As you dig deeper, you will usually find that there is one type that best describes you. When you work through the questionnaires in most Enneagram books, you will find that you score high on some types and low on others.

You can get a preliminary indication of your Enneagram type using the questionnaire on the EnneaSurvey website (www.EnneaSurvey.com). I recommend using this questionnaire as part of a process of elimination by discarding your low-scoring types and digging deeper into the others.

## Embracing All Perspectives

Because I am Type 6, at the core of the thinking center, my typical behaviors can be hyperrational. Behaviors based on intuition (such as those in the intuitive center) or behaviors based on feelings (such as those in the feeling center) can seem irrational to me. One of the biggest benefits I have personally received from the Enneagram is the understanding that rationality is simply not that important to most other types, and that there are legitimate, alternative perspectives that I can learn to appreciate. This realization has enabled me to value these perspectives and understand the importance and unique contributions of each Enneagram type to the greater good of the team and the community. This is the most important thing I have learned from studying the Enneagram.

In the next section we will discuss another distinguishing aspect of the Enneagram: the paths of integration and disintegration. These paths describe how our behaviors change as our security and stress levels change. Each type has a unique pair of paths, and you can use these paths to distinguish among the types. But, before that, a short paragraph on one-word descriptions.

## One-Word Descriptions

As you can imagine, each type is much more complex than can be described with a single word. While these one-word labels are instructive when first learning the Enneagram, you are apt to start calling the types simply by their number once you have mastered the nine types. The number label is neutral and can convey a type's characteristics without overemphasizing any one trait. In the type number illustrations, we have attempted to capture the essence of each Enneagram type, particularly in its relationship to problem solving. In subsequent chapters, I will simply use the type number to describe each Enneagram type.

# Paths of Integration and Disintegration

The paths of integration and disintegration are features that distinguish the Enneagram from other personality typing systems. These paths serve as a tool to understand the broad range of behaviors exhibited by any one type. The following descriptions serve as a refresher to those familiar with the Enneagram and highlight certain behavioral characteristics important to problem solving that will be discussed in later chapters.

Referring to the Enneagram diagram, you will notice lines connecting the numbers. These lines are called the paths of integration and disintegration. The direction of the path of integration is indicated by the arrows. The path of disintegration is the opposite direction.

The Enneagram is not a static system; it does not describe a person as a fixed type. Behaviors associated with a specific type can change over time and under different circumstances, depending on whether we are secure, insecure, or at baseline. The paths of integration (towards security) and disintegration (towards insecurity) describe these changes in behavior.

For example, these paths describe how our behaviors change between the time when we are young and immature (less integrated) and adult and mature (more integrated). As we become adults, most of us learn to temper our behaviors. Because of this, some Enneagram texts will advise people who are trying to identify their own Enneagram type to recall their behaviors in their mid-twenties because that is when they are most likely acting in their baseline and less integrated states.

As adults, we may find our levels of integration and disintegration vary due to stress. We may even notice our own behavioral changes, depending on circumstances. These circumstances drive our movement along these paths of integration and disintegration, and our behaviors vary accordingly. The Enneagram describes remarkably well how our behaviors change.

Each Enneagram type is connected to two other types by these paths. The core types (3, 6, and 9) are connected by a triangle. One direction around the triangle, clockwise, represents the path of integration; the counterclockwise direction represents disintegration.

### Core (Suppressed Response) Types
Path of Integration: 3→6→9→3
Path of Disintegration: 3→9→6→3

The remaining, non-core types are connected in the following way:

### Internal and External Response Types
Path of Integration: 1→7→5→8→2→4→1
Path of Disintegration: 1→4→2→8→5→7→1

The following are brief descriptions of behaviors of each type traversing the paths of integration or disintegration. Note how the behaviors can change dramatically, yet the underlying motivation for each type remains constant. Conversely, note how the behaviors for two different types can be remarkably similar, but the motivations for those similar behaviors are different.

**Path of Integration: Type 1 → Type 7.** As Type 1s release their innate desire to right the wrongs that they see, they relieve themselves of their sense of frustration and begin expressing a playful, fun-seeking side of their personality—behavior typical of Type 7. When the 1 goes on vacation, figuratively or literally, so does their angry, critical inner voice. The absence of this critical inner voice allows their playful side to emerge, often surprising those around them.

**Path of Disintegration: Type 1 → Type 4.** As the 1s become overwhelmed with frustration, they can enter a state resembling that of Type 4. The constant harping of the critical inner voice can put the 1 into a state that resembles depression. Under those circumstances, the 1s can redirect the inner voice outward, usually targeting a person with whom they are intimate. The targeted person would then be on the receiving end of that critical voice and would hear an outpouring, in list-like detail, of everything that has bothered the 1 about them, often going far back in time.

**Path of Integration: Type 2 → Type 4.** When the 2s quiet their desire to connect emotionally with others, it opens the space for them to engage with their own feelings. Their focus turns inward, and they become introspective, resembling Type 4 in their connection to their own feelings. In this state, the 2s are able to spend time alone and to engage in activities that interest them—often artistic in nature—without the need to engage with others.

**Path of Disintegration: Type 2 → Type 8.** For the 2s, appreciation can be like oxygen. They need a constant flow; otherwise, they feel like they are suffocating. There are situations when 2s may feel entitled to appreciation they don't receive. For instance, Type 2s may try to help people who did not ask for or want help, and their well-intentioned but misplaced efforts are unlikely to receive the expected gratitude. When the 2s feel underappreciated, neglected, or taken for granted, they can exhibit assertive, aggressive behaviors characteristic of Type 8, thrusting themselves more forcefully into the situation. In this state, 2s can lose their sense of boundaries with others, which can further aggravate the situation.

**Path of Integration: Type 3 → Type 6.** As the 3s release their need for recognition and acknowledgment of their successes, they enter a quiet state that allows them to broaden their perspective and horizon. In this state, the 3s can "work smarter, not harder" and pursue their productive ends with systematic efficiency, resembling the behavior of Type 6. In this state, a 3 is also able to think through and appreciate the reactions and feelings of others as well as how their own behaviors and words affect them.

**Path of Disintegration: Type 3 → Type 9.** The 3s feel most threatened when they lose sight of their path to success and their opportunities for recognition. Under those circumstances, their first instinct is to focus acutely on looking for opportunities to appease the people around them—behavior typical of Type 9. If still unable to achieve success through appeasement, the 3 will withdraw from the situation entirely, also typical of Type 9 withdrawal from a highly contentious situation.

**Path of Integration: Type 4 → Type 1.** As 4s develop, they establish for themselves principles based on truth and beauty. Once these principles have been established, the 4s can use them as guideposts for decision making and behavior, moving beyond simply reacting to their feelings in the moment. As 4s move towards principles-based decision making, they exhibit a style similar to that of the principled Type 1 in their interactions with others.

**Path of Disintegration: Type 4 → Type 2.** When the 4's feelings overwhelm them, those feelings can pour out. They lose their typical calm demeanor as the wall between the outside world and their internal feelings breaks down. When this happens, the 4 exhibits overtly emotional and dramatic behaviors that can resemble those of Type 2.

**Path of Integration: Type 5 → Type 8.** As they build up their realm of expertise and as their fear of appearing ignorant subsides, the 5s can take on the confident demeanor of the 8s, who are unafraid to communicate and advocate for their ideas. In their secure state, Type 5s can assume leadership roles much like Type 8s do.

**Path of Disintegration: Type 5 → Type 7.** While the typical state of the 5s is the quiet observer, when thrust into a situation where people's attention turns to them and they cannot escape, their minds start racing. The energy of the racing mind resembles that of the typical frenetic Type 7, and the 5s can become nervous and chatty under those circumstances.

**Path of Integration: Type 6 → Type 9.** As the 6s become calm, anxiety recedes—unmasking senses that previously have been overwhelmed. In this state, the 6s become more aware of the feelings, needs, and wants of people around them, and they integrate that awareness into their thinking. In this way, the 6s begin to resemble Type 9 in their sensitivity to others' needs and desires.

**Path of Disintegration: Type 6 → Type 3.** Conversely, as anxiety levels rise, the senses of the 6s become increasingly overwhelmed. Under these circumstances, the 6 becomes hyperfocused on addressing the source of their anxiety, often at the expense of the feelings of other people. This focused pursuit of a task at hand without consideration of others around them resembles behaviors of Type 3.

**Path of Integration: Type 7 → Type 5.** As their incessant need to determine how they stand with others subsides, the 7s are free to quietly pursue activities that interest them. These activities are often motivated by intellectual curiosity. This independent pursuit of their own interests resembles the baseline behavior of the 5.

**Path of Disintegration: Type 7 → Type 1.** When the 7s are in a particularly anxiety-inducing situation, the happy, fun-seeking demeanor fades and the 7s can take on a serious, intense, and narrowly focused position without considering what others are thinking of them. They can stay in this state until the situation is resolved and the wrong is righted. In this state, the 7's behavior resembles that of the 1.

**Path of Integration: Type 8 → Type 2.** Once 8s have secured their own environment and situation, they begin to consider the situations and security of others around them, especially people within their domain or under their protection. The 8s have a tremendous capacity for action as well as considerable energy to devote to aiding others. When they shift into these roles, their behaviors begin to resemble those of Type 2.

**Path of Disintegration: Type 8 → Type 5.** When Type 8s feel threatened, they become laser-focused on assessing the threat and identifying its weaknesses. Once they have formulated how best to attack the threat, they do it with mighty force. Prior to the attack, as they assess the threatening situation, the 8s can appear like the quietly observing Type 5—or like a crouching tiger preparing to attack.

**Path of Integration: Type 9 → Type 3.** When the 9 senses that the people in their environment are at peace, they can redirect their considerable energy towards contributing to the greater good and success of their team or their community. This behavior can make the 9s look like the highly productive and successful Type 3 in their behavior.

**Path of Disintegration: Type 9 → Type 6.** As discord in the environment increases, overwhelming their ability to cope with conflicts, the 9 can become passive-aggressive and/or disengaged. Sometimes, they withdraw completely. In this state, the 9's behavior resembles that of the Type 6 when they refuse to go along with everyone else.

# Understanding Type Dynamics

As you can see, Enneagram types can exhibit a wide variety of behavior depending on whether they are in their typical baseline state, their integrated secure state, or their stressful insecure state. The paths of integration and disintegration are a great tool for understanding these shifts in behavior and identifying the state or "mood" of those around us, allowing us to be more understanding of their particular situation. When people act out in unusual ways, it often has less to do with the immediate situation and more to do with some other stress in their lives. Understanding how people might act out when they are under stress can give us the perspective and patience to better accommodate and mitigate those behaviors.

---

## Relationships

---

When I was beginning my studies of the Enneagram, I stumbled on the website (www.enneagraminstitute.com) for the Enneagram Institute. On this site, there was a link to a section called "Compatibility with Other Types," describing relationships among the various types. That section is still there at the time of this writing, and it can be found by clicking on the description of any type and then scrolling down towards the bottom of the page. Once I determined my type and the type of my wife, I went to the relevant webpage and read the descriptions for the "healthy," "normal," and "unhealthy" states of our relationship. I was stunned at how remarkably well those sections described our interactions in these three states, as if the writer knew us personally. This was yet another epiphany for me about the capabilities of the Enneagram to predict and describe interpersonal dynamics among types.

**The Identity Mirror**

# Trouble Self-Identifying?
# Try Looking into the Identity Mirror!

Still having trouble identifying your Enneagram type? In my experience, some Enneagram types have more trouble self-identifying than others (see Table 1.2). Over the years, I have collected scenarios that I use to help people determine their Enneagram type. I call this the *Identity Mirror*. Below I share some of my favorite Identity Mirror stories. Try putting yourself into each of these scenarios and think about what you would do. Perhaps you will see yourself in one of these scenarios reacting in the manner typical of your Enneagram type.

### Table 1.2 – Enneagram Self-Identification

| Type | Self-Identification |
|:---:|:---:|
| 1 | Easier |
| 2 | Harder |
| 3 | Easier |
| 4 | Harder |
| 5 | Harder |
| 6 | Harder |
| 7 | Variable – Can Be Easier or Harder |
| 8 | Easier |
| 9 | Harder |

**Type 1s** typically have an easy time identifying themselves. They identify with the frustration in the struggle to "get it right."

**Type 1 Identity Mirror.** Imagine that you are printing out a forty-page report and the printer runs out of paper on the last page. You reload the printer with new paper and print out the last page. As you assemble the report, you notice that the last page has an ever-so-slightly different shade of white paper than the rest of the report. What would you do? If you are Type 1, the answer is obvious: reprint the entire report.

**Type 2s** often struggle with identifying themselves. They are so tuned to considering the feelings of others that they have trouble examining their own feelings. They will even have trouble identifying that they are driven by feelings.

**Type 2 Identity Mirror.** Being the external emotion type, Type 2 wants an emotional connection with another person. This desire drives the 2 to interact with others. Curiously, if you ask Type 2s whether they need time alone, they will often say yes. If asked when they last spent time alone, they may have to think about it a while before they respond, if they can remember at all. Then, if you ask them how long they spent alone, they may say something like "30 minutes." For the 2, spending 30 minutes without being around someone else can seem like a long time. I have noticed that Type 2s who live alone often have pets in order to fulfill the need for emotional connection and companionship.

**Type 3s** tend to self-identify easily. They look at the type descriptions, and they resonate with the type who is pursuing success and working hard to get it.

**Type 3 Identity Mirror.** Many people have clothes strewn about their bedroom—usually dirty clothes we have not yet put in the hamper. If you're Type 3, the clothes strewn on your bed are likely clean! As the 3 starts their day, they try on different outfits and imagine the impact each will make on the people they expect to meet (and impress) that day. By the time they achieve the desired look, they are often running late and don't have time to put everything away.

**Type 4s** may have an easier time self-identifying, although they may not want to share their identity with others for fear of making themselves more

emotionally vulnerable than they already feel. Generally, they are putting up a front in order to mask all the emotions they are feeling all the time.

**Type 4 Identity Mirror.** Type 4s tend to pine for what is missing, and as such the death of a loved one, or even a beloved pet, will often affect them deeply. They may grieve much longer than other types would expect. They often connect more deeply with books or films that include powerful death scenes. If you find yourself drawn to situations that evoke powerful emotions and pining for things missing in your life, then you may be a 4.

**Type 5s** have a harder time self-identifying. They are masters at assuming roles, depending on the environment and circumstances. They can often develop different personas—one for work, one for home, and one for friends. They may confuse these personas for their true nature since the 5 feels they can play the role of any of the types. Once the 5 self-identifies, they may be uncomfortable sharing that information with others since they are generally the least willing of all types to share personal information.

**Type 5 Identity Mirror.** The Observer 5 spends the day quietly absorbing information from the environment. In the evening before sleep, the 5 will relive the day, mentally replaying all the details. If you find yourself doing this consistently every day, you are likely a 5.

**Type 6s** tend to be reluctant to self-identify, though the behavior of the 6 is usually apparent to others around them. Since many of the natural behaviors of the 6 can seem negative—like worrying, questioning everything, and being skeptical—the 6 often refrains from their natural instincts in order to better fit in with the group. They deliberately

turn their pessimism into optimism as they look to the "bright side" or the "realistic" side. Their instinctive reluctance to act may turn to overconfidence or bluster. These behaviors help the 6 fit in and mask underlying anxiety.

**Type 6 Identity Mirror.** Type 6 has a propensity to say no to a new idea, even before they have taken time to consider it. This immediate reaction is a safety mechanism. Curiously, the 6 may say no even when they want to say yes and will experience an immediate feeling of regret. If you find yourself automatically saying no to new ideas, then you are probably a 6.

**Type 7s** may go either way with self-identification. Most commonly, they easily identify with their type since they resonate with the fun, talkativeness, and enthusiasm associated with the type. The other pattern I see is that 7s perceive the Enneagram type identification as a box, and they resist being put in a box.

**Type 7 Identity Mirror.** Type 7s abhor delivering bad news. They like keeping things light, fun, and positive. If they ever have to convey bad news, they deliver it as a *compliment sandwich,* layered between two compliments or positive thoughts. Often the recipients of such news are confused with this delivery, not quite knowing how to react. If you struggle to get to the point and deliver bad news without embedding it within other, happier conversations, then you are probably a 7.

**Type 8s** tend to self-identify easily. They resonate with the sense of confidence of the 8. Also, they easily recognize in themselves the direct, straightforward approach that the 8 uses to address situations.

**Type 8 Identity Mirror.** At times Type 8s will display anger, or so it seems to those around them. But the 8s themselves do not necessarily feel angry or confrontational in any way. They are "just having a conversation." This pattern is common with the 8s; most 8s will say they have had the experience of people asking them why they are angry when they do not feel that they are.

**Type 9s** have trouble with self-identification. They are constantly putting themselves in others' shoes and imagining how others will react. When doing this, it is easy for 9s to lose their own sense of self. As the 9s explore the types, they see themselves in each, making it hard for them to land on just one.

**Type 9 Identity Mirror.** When 9s first awake, they immediately start processing how they are going to minimize conflicts during the day. They want to avoid conflict at home, at work, and at any planned activities. If you find yourself preparing to minimize conflict from the moment you awake, you are likely a 9.

# A Word on Wings

In Enneagram parlance, *wings* are the numbers on either side of each Enneagram type. For instance, if you are Type 9, then your wings are Type 1 and Type 8. Wings can provide insight into behavioral variations in the types that may not be explained by the paths of integration and disintegration. For example, I use wings as a tool for understanding introversion and extroversion tendencies for each type. In the example of Type 9, some 9s are more outgoing and are said to have an 8 wing. Others are more introverted, and those are said to have a 1 wing. The pattern that one of the wings is more extroverted and one more introverted holds true in large part for all the types.

## Other Triads

The Enneagram's main triads—(8-9-1), (2-3-4), and (5-6-7)—were described in some detail in this chapter. But there are two other sets of triads that we will explore in Chapter 7, "Work Team Triads: Two Balanced Brains":

Temperament triads:     (3-7-8), (1-2-6), and (4-5-9)
Harmony triads:         (1-4-7), (2-5-8), and (3-6-9)

We will return to these triads in the context of building effective work teams.

## Summary

Now that you understand the Enneagram types, you are ready to see how these nine puzzle pieces fit together to form the foundation for team-based problem solving. Understanding the Enneagram types of the individuals on your team, including yourself, is an important piece of this puzzle. This chapter is not intended to be a primer on the Enneagram. My purpose is to introduce the vocabulary of the Enneagram and to highlight the dynamics that each type contributes to team-based problem solving.

Having conversations with others about the Enneagram types is a great way to understand these nine dynamics and see them in action. TV and film are also a terrific playground to observe these dynamics. *The Wizard of Oz* is particularly poignant to me because it illustrates the Enneagram's three centers. For those curious, I place the cowardly Lion as Type 6, who aspires to be a courageous leader like a person in the Gut-Intuitive-Anger center; Type 6 has access to this along their path of integration to Type 9. The Tin Man is the suppressed emotion Type 3—core type of the Heart-Feeling-Emotion center—who strives to get in touch with feelings. And the Scarecrow is the affable Type 7—Head-Thinking-Anxiety center—who, by wanting a brain, represents movement along the path of integration towards the contemplative Type 5. As for Dorothy, I see her as the unflappable Type 9, facing every challenge with consideration, composure, and only a little bit of anger when really, really pushed. (Spoiler alert: Most of the film depicts Dorothy while she is sleeping—classic 9 behavior!)

The next chapter (Chapter 2, "Problem Solving with the Enneagram") explains a framework I developed that puts these puzzle pieces together. Using this framework, you will be able to propel your team towards its goals.

**CHAPTER 2**

# Problem Solving
# with the Enneagram

I started working at Palm Inc. a little over a year after Palm had acquired Handspring. The group I managed had about fifty people. Roughly half were originally with Palm and half had come from Handspring. My predecessors—one from Palm, the other from Handspring—each had a turn leading the hardware development group since the merger. Under these two managers, the original Palm and Handspring groups became even more adversarial. Both sides were acutely aware of this divide and had begun calling themselves Boot Camp (Palm) and Woodstock (Handspring). Management brought me in specifically because I was not affiliated with either group.

Coming into this contentious situation, I needed a tool to bring these factions together and focus them on solving problems instead of pointing fingers. This environment provided the perfect opportunity to deploy my Enneagram-based approach to problem solving.

# The Sum Is Greater Than the Parts

In the last chapter (Chapter 1, "The Enneagram Briefly"), we explored the nine Enneagram dynamics. In this chapter, I describe the problem-solving framework I developed based on those nine dynamics. This framework provides a platform for deeply understanding teams and the dynamics in play when people work together to solve problems.

There are certain tasks in problem solving at which we each excel and others where we do not perform as strongly. The nine Enneagram dynamics describe a set of talents that serves well at each specific step in problem solving. When we combine our talents, our collective ability exceeds the sum of the individual abilities, creating *synergism*—the Aristotelian concept that the whole is greater than the sum of its parts. The Enneagram serves as the platform to build synergistic work teams.

# The Enneagram-Based Problem-Solving Methodology

My exploration of Enneagram-based problem solving began with a simple question: The Enneagram numbers imply an order, so why is the Perfectionist the 1, the Helper 2, the Achiever 3, and so on? The order seemed arbitrary. For instance, why couldn't the whole circle be rotated so that the Perfectionist is Type 3? One of my Enneagram mentors told me that the specific order of the Enneagram types is important and referred me to a book by Klausbernd Vollmar.

Vollmar's book, *The Secret of Enneagrams: Mapping the Personality*, asserts that the Enneagram describes flows of energies. He goes on to explain that there is a specific sequence to those energy flows in the numerical order of the Enneagram types.

Having a background in science and engineering, I have used many different problem-solving methods such as the scientific method. I noticed a pattern between the steps in problem-solving methods and the numerical order of the dynamics of the Enneagram. The Enneagram numbers describe the order of the steps by which humans solve problems. With that epiphany, the number assignments on the Enneagram now made perfect sense.

Using the language of problem solving, the dynamics associated with each Enneagram type can be described as follows:

**Step 1: Problem-Goal.** Identify the problems and define the goals.

**Step 2: Stakeholder Identification.** Recruit a committed team.

**Step 3: Ideation.** Generate ideas for solutions.

**Step 4: Emotional Reaction.** Assess reactions to each idea.

**Step 5: Logical Analysis.** Study and score promising ideas.

**Step 6: Planning.** Select the most promising idea and build an action plan.

**Step 7: Promotion.** Passionately promote the plan and get approval to proceed.

**Step 8: Implementation.** Execute the plan and solve the problem!

**Step 9: Integration.** Confirm the problem is solved with all stakeholders.

Using the Enneagram as a framework for solving problems highlights how each Enneagram type is attuned to a particular step in the problem-solving process. There is a one-to-one mapping between the Enneagram types and the steps in the process. It seems that humans instinctively know how to solve problems as a team, and the Enneagram describes that methodology.

While at Palm, I used my Enneagram-based methodology to facilitate a number of cross-functional problem-solving initiatives. The Enneagram-based approach worked remarkably well despite the fractious environment.

Our first initiative tackled integrating accessory product development with the main product development effort. The Enneagram problem-solving method effectively aligned various factions into a coherent problem-solving team. Our first effort was so successful that our executive sponsor encouraged me to continue with additional initiatives, including the main product development process, product lifecycle management, compliance, and product quality initiatives.

These initiatives required the participation of team members from across the organization, including engineering, quality, operations, procurement, legal, finance, and others. As people from across the organization worked together, the divisions between former Palm and Handspring employees dissolved. The Enneagram-based approach proved perfectly suited to aligning a diverse group of leaders to address challenges that broadly affected the organization.

In this chapter, I show how you can take your team through the Enneagram-based problem-solving methodology. I describe each problem-solving step in turn and explain how the dynamics of each Enneagram type contribute to group problem solving. Also, I provide insights and techniques for facilitating your work teams at each step.

As a context for these descriptions, imagine that you are charged with tackling a large challenge for your organization that requires the participation of multiple team members, much like I experienced at Palm. A sponsor who recognizes that the organization must overcome the challenge to become more successful—perhaps a board member or an executive at the company—convenes the team. You are coordinating a cross-functional group of leaders within the organization that is being impacted by the problem and are charged with fixing it.

Although I use this example to explain the methodology, the process can be used for any group of people—a product development group, a community-based group, a political policy group—that is coming together to collectively solve a common problem.

# The Problem-Solving Wheel

This methodology for work team problem solving can be viewed as a wheel which rolls forward through each step in the problem-solving process. Like a wheel, this methodology is an efficient tool to move teams forward. Once a team is in motion it wants to stay in motion. Conversely, once it gets stuck it takes effort to get it rolling again. Balance is required for smooth operation; if it's out of balance, the ride will be bumpy. The wheel will serve as our metaphor to describe the motion of the team through the problem-solving process.

# Step 1: Problem-Goal

## *So, What's the Problem?*

The first step in problem solving is where the energy of Enneagram Type 1 shines. Type 1 is acutely attuned to identifying and communicating the existence of problems. This dynamic is exactly what is needed in Step 1 of problem solving in order to clearly define the problem.

When a problem affects multiple groups in an organization—development, operations, finance, customer support, marketing, etc.—it can have a devastating impact on the organization's effectiveness. A common awareness of the problem can serve as an impetus for action and change. In such circumstances, I find it beneficial to take the time to get input from all constituents and to document the problem from each group's perspective. When it's done together in a meeting or over lunch, you will find that this step has the added benefit of team building too.

It is important that the team take the time to thoroughly document the problem. Many teams do not take this action, but without it the team may end up solving a completely different problem—or not solving any problem at all. Unless you document the problem, your problem-solving wheel will end up off track.

On the other hand, taking the time to clearly document the problem helps your team stay focused on addressing it. The problem descriptions can also serve as your metrics for success. In the end, you can assess how well your team solved the problem by comparing the solution to the original problem descriptions.

In Step 1, Type 1s are not the only contributors. It is important for all team members to embrace the dynamic of Type 1 and to describe the problem as they see it. If a problem has persisted for a long time, the affected people may have started to blame one another. In Step 1, you need to rise above finger-pointing and record the problem descriptions objectively, just as they are shared.

### *The Elephant in the Room*

A large problem can seem like an elephant. Some people will describe the smell. Some will describe the noise. Some feel like they are being crushed or squeezed. People focus on the symptoms and effects— how they personally experience the problem. At some point, your team members begin to appreciate that, although the symptoms they personally experience may be different, the root cause of the various symptoms is the same: there is an elephant in the room. Once the team recognizes that they all share a common problem—a common enemy, so to speak—the team shifts from focusing on one another to focusing on that common enemy.

In my practice as a team facilitator, I invite the team members to a kickoff meeting at the outset of a problem-solving initiative. This meeting is the first of two meetings for Step 1. I encourage everyone to vent about the problem, describing the problem as they see it and the troubles the problem causes them. This meeting can quickly become animated as everyone chimes in and describes their unique point of view while I frantically scribble comments on flip charts. Everyone has the opportunity to hear and understand everyone else's perspective on the problem. During Step 1, it is especially important to allow those who feel victimized by the problem to elaborate on those feelings and the impacts they are suffering. Sharing each other's perspectives builds understanding and empathy among team members.

**Recognizing the Common Problem**

## *The Common Problem*

What is happening in this first team meeting? I have noticed several things. Firstly, everyone is allowed the opportunity to vent, and that venting is a cathartic process in and of itself. Secondly, the team members start to appreciate each other's perspectives, building empathy. Thirdly, the team starts to recognize the common problem they all share—rather than blaming one another for the problem, the team members are now focused on their common enemy. And finally, a sense of excitement and anticipation grows about embarking collectively on a journey to overcome that common enemy. These outcomes enable the participants to become a cohesive problem-solving team.

**Visualizing the Beautiful World**

## *The Beautiful World*

The flip side of the terrible world is the beautiful world, the world in which the big common problem has been eliminated. Once everyone has had a chance to describe the problem in the first meeting, I adjourn the group and reconvene on the following day. At the second meeting, I ask every stakeholder in turn to describe that beautiful world and how it will improve their situation. This technique is called *visualizing*, and it creates a focal point for the group as they work through the subsequent steps in the problem-solving process.

Some people find it more natural to complain about the existing world than to envision a beautiful new world. Some will even revert to complaining about the problem because it is easier for them. Certainly, if they are introducing new aspects of the problem unaired the previous day, these need to be recorded. On the other hand, if they are simply rehashing issues already raised, you need to encourage them to look beyond the current situation and describe their future beautiful world. You can do this by simply asking, "So, how *should* it be?"

"Should" is a word often used in the dynamic of Type 1. It is clear to 1s how the world should be, and Step 1 is the time to tap into that energy. When everyone is encouraged to describe their vision of the beautiful world, themes will begin to emerge. These themes will serve as the goals your team uses to formulate the metrics for success.

## Homework: Goals and Metrics

In my practice, I organize the themes that emerge from the second meeting into the goals for the team. Also, where possible, I quantify outcomes to establish metrics for success. As homework for the team, I distribute the goals and metrics to them for review, comment, and prioritization. I collect their comments and suggestions and incorporate those into our team goals. This document serves as the guide for the initiative.

---

### OK about OKRs—But Why, Who, What, and How?

---

OKR stands for Objectives and Key Results. OKRs are a simple tool organizations use to record and share objectives and keep track of progress towards meeting those objectives. OKRs were popularized by Intel and have spread throughout Silicon Valley. For instance, they are regularly used at Google, among other companies.

OKRs clearly speak to the quantification of goals. What they lack is an elucidation of the problem itself. While problem-goal may be two sides of the same coin, there is value to elaborating both. Without a clear description of the problem, the *why* of the objective can be lost. Those using OKRs may want to consider a modified version: POKR—Problem, Objective, Key Results.

Further, the OKR system does not inform you of the *who, what, how,* and *when* related to your objectives. The Enneagram methodology considers all these aspects. For more details, read on.

---

# Step 2: Stakeholder Identification

The next step in your problem-solving initiative is to pull together the team of people committed to solving the problem and realizing the vision of the beautiful world. Enneagram Type 2s are attuned to understanding the emotional connections that people have with the problem and with one another. They intuitively know who will benefit by eliminating the problem and thereby who will have an emotional stake in the problem-solving effort. Step 2 in the problem-solving process involves tapping into Type 2's dynamic and recruiting team members who are passionate about solving the problem.

A few days after the Step 1 kickoff meetings, I hold a Step 2 meeting. I review the goals the team formulated and ensure that everyone is satisfied with the scope and wording. This process can take a little time, and I wait for the team to get it *just right.*

Next, press your team to think through who they need to accomplish the goals. This activity is the heart of Step 2. Who needs to be involved in the initiative from beginning to end? Were other people identified during the Step 1 meetings who are impacted by the problem in some way? If so, you should consider including them on the team. Is certain expertise required to solve the problem? If so, you should enlist the help of those experts. Will there be an impact on the workflow of any group or groups while solving the problem? If so, make sure those groups are represented. How about a need for systems or IT infrastructure? If yes, include an IT representative as part of your group.

Simply put, ensure that the people who need to be involved in both designing the solution and living with the results are represented on your team. These people are your stakeholders.

**The Committed Team**

## Roles and Responsibilities

Take time to ensure that every team member understands their role in the initiative. Before meeting with the entire team, I instruct all participants to think about how they will contribute. At the meeting, I have each member describe their contribution plan, and I document what each team member says. This document becomes the Roles and

Responsibilities charter for the team. By the end of this meeting, you should have a clear description of each team member's role and the area for which they will take responsibility. Those who do not feel they have a stake in the initiative will tend to bow out at this point. Importantly, everyone remaining on the team will have heard everyone else's commitments to both the team and the initiative.

## Housekeeping

If you add new members to your team after the Step 1 problem-goal meetings, loop back with the new team members and record the problems as described from their perspectives. If any new problems are aired, record them and share them with the team. You will also want to add to or adjust the initiative's goals to ensure that the new problems are addressed. By including input from your new team members, you ensure that they feel vested in the process.

## Check In with the Sponsor

Once you have identified your team members and articulated their roles and responsibilities, check in with your sponsor again. Remember that you are helping the sponsor. In the spirit of the Type 2 Helper dynamic, you need to ensure that the team is on track to solve the problem as envisioned by the sponsor. Vet the problem-goal statement with the sponsor to ensure that the team's goals and the sponsor's goals are aligned. Also, confirm that the sponsor endorses the team members' commitments and allocation of resources to the initiative. Once you are satisfied that there is alignment and support, you are ready to proceed to Step 3: Ideation.

# Step 3: Ideation

Now that you have described your problem in detail, envisioned your goal, and assembled your committed team, you are ready to explore ideas for solving the problem.

By the time you arrive at this point in the process, your team members will likely already have begun chiming in with ideas about how to solve the problem. This is one natural indication that you have arrived at Step 3, the Ideation phase of problem solving. In this step you capture briefly as many ideas as possible in what I call the *Ideathon*. In this step, you capture briefly as many ideas as possible. No idea is "bad" or "impossible." An idea is just an idea. In practice, I find that the more generous you are in allowing ideas, the more it inspires your team to generate even more ideas. Be a generous listener and collect them all.

**Ideation**

Everyone has ideas, so what makes the Enneagram Type 3 dynamic particularly suited for this step? Remember, the 3 is the core type of the Heart-Feeling-Emotion center and thus *suppresses* emotion. For those of us who do not suppress emotion, our emotions act as filters on our thoughts. We judge emotionally whether an idea is "good" or "bad." Our emotional connection with others might inhibit the expression of an idea for fear of how they may respond.

Imagine if you had no emotional baggage associated with any particular idea. Imagine if your ideas weren't influenced by what others think or how they might respond. Imagine a space where you could express any idea that came to mind, without inhibitions. This is exactly what's required at this point in problem solving, and that is the space of the Type 3 dynamic.

## What Is an Idea?

An idea is any thought. It may be a big, complex thought, or it may be a simple thought. It may have come up before, or it may be newly minted. It may be funny, serious, or even impossible. All thoughts and all ideas are welcome in Step 3. The ideation session is a chance for the group to flex its creative muscle. Encourage your team to explore boundaries, jump over them, and expand beyond them as much as possible.

## The Warm-Up Exercise

A dear friend and mentor once encouraged me to start each ideation session with a warm-up exercise. Once she had us imagine the similarities between a refrigerator and a cat. This is still my favorite warm-up question. My favorite answer to date is that both are endothermic—in other words, they both give off heat. That is the perfect answer for a "warm-up" exercise! No matter how many times I ask this question, I hear original ideas from each new group of people, which reminds me to always include ideas from diverse team members with varying backgrounds and experiences.

## *The Ideathon*

After the warm-up exercise, I have the team generate ideas for accomplishing each goal and solving its related problems. I have the team consider both the goal and the problem since each view may expose different ideas. I ensure that each problem-goal pair is allotted time for ideation. For instance, if there are 10 problem-goal pairs and 50 minutes, I will ensure that the team starts the transition to the next pair after 5 minutes.

Intentionally, this session quickly becomes a high-energy meeting with many ideas being bandied about. I will stand at the flip chart, scribbling down each idea as it is aired—no filters! For instance, if multiple people voice the same idea, I will capture that idea multiple times.

Some people will be natural contributors in this environment. Some will not. The "naturals" will chime in without much prodding, but those who are quiet also have important contributions that must be aired. After the initial idea frenzy, I will go around the room and ensure that each person has had an opportunity to contribute a thought or two. I also remind people that some ideas may occur after the meeting and encourage them to share those ideas too. The point is to get as many different ideas into the mix as possible.

## *Sugar!*

To keep the energy levels high, I serve tasty, sugar-laden treats for the team to enjoy. While I usually do not prioritize the problems and the order in which each is addressed, I do try to leave the less difficult problems for later in the meeting, in case the team starts to run out of steam. Since sugar can only take you so far, the longest I would advise conducting this type of ideation session is 90 minutes.

## Yes, And ...

There is a technique used in improvisational comedy called "Yes, and ..." Using this technique enables an improv team to maintain a continuous flow of original ideas and take the comedy sketch in many interesting and creative directions. During the ideation session, I encourage participants to use "Yes, and ..." to keep up a positive flow of ideas. No "Nos," no "Buts," and no objections—just "Yes, ... and"!

## The Idea Space

At the end of this session, you will have a rich set of ideas to work with. You will have allowed all your team members to contribute and to appreciate each other's contributions. Done well, the ideation session energizes the team and increases team morale. The interactions also generate hope. The team sees possibilities for solving the problems and reaching the goals.

In the next two steps, your team will scrutinize each idea and assess its viability. We perform two types of assessment: emotional reaction and logical analysis. First, we examine emotional reaction—Step 4 in problem solving.

# Step 4: Emotional Reaction

What is the first thing that happens when you hear a new idea? You have an emotional reaction. That idea is great! Or, that idea stinks! People inevitably have an emotional reaction to any idea. This emotional reaction corresponds to the dynamic of Enneagram Type 4. The reaction happens subconsciously and instantaneously and can guide much of our thinking thereafter. These first reactions are important to problem solving, and the team needs to pay attention to them.

**First Reactions**

At the beginning of the ideation session (Step 3), I explain the first-reaction phenomenon to the participants and acknowledge that they will likely experience it. I instruct them that if they have a positive reaction to an idea it is OK to express it. On the other hand, if they have a negative reaction to an idea, then I ask that they hold their thought and think about why they are having that negative reaction. Once they understand why, then I suggest they redirect that negative energy in a positive direction and imagine an idea more suitable to them. I encourage them to simply share their new idea with the group without objecting to the previous idea.

Think of this technique as *idea jujitsu*. In other words, have team members rechannel the negative energy from their reaction into a positive idea they can share with the group. This technique is related to the spirit of "Yes, and …," described above, and will maintain the flow of fresh, new ideas. In this way, the team can maintain a high energy level and a positive tone for the duration of the ideation session.

Since emotional reactions to ideas are instantaneous, in practice I find it necessary to conduct Steps 3 and 4 (Ideation and Emotional Reaction) simultaneously. By having team members process their emotional reactions during the ideation session, I find that the group will naturally migrate towards the promising ideas—those ideas with a positive emotional response. The group will tend to elaborate on the ideas that generate the most positive energy. That positive energy will carry into Step 5 in which the team carefully scrutinizes the most promising ideas.

## *Mind the Gap: Step 4 to Step 5*

Recalling the paths of integration and disintegration, you will see that Enneagram Type 4 is connected to both Types 1 and 2. These connections exert an influence on problem solving and on your team. At this point in the problem-solving process, there will be a tendency for your team to move backwards, wanting to revisit the activities of Steps 1 and 2. It will be important for you to recognize if this happens and to keep the team on track and moving forward across the gap from Step 4 to Step 5.

# Step 5: Logical Analysis

The transition to Step 5 represents a movement away from emotion-based processing towards logic-based thinking. Enneagram Type 5 is in the Head-Thinking-Anxiety center and the Enneagram dynamic best suited for data collection and detailed analysis.

Recall that Enneagram Type 5 is the internal anxiety type concerned with accumulating resources. This behavior extends to collecting information, making the Type 5 dynamic ideally suited for gathering all the data necessary to properly analyze each idea. With the data at hand, your team can perform cost-benefit analyses, generating the facts crucial to deciding which ideas are most viable for achieving the objectives and solving the problem. During Step 5, your problem-solving team must move into the Type 5 dynamic, carefully and logically analyzing all the promising ideas.

**Analysis**

## *Analysis, Not Paralysis*

Most ideas have their good points and bad points and their pros and cons. It is important for you to move your problem-solving team quickly through the assessment of these pros and cons. If you call a 100-minute team meeting and you have 12 big ideas to examine, keep the pro/con analysis of each idea to 8 minutes. You will find that your team is usually able to discuss the important points of each idea in those 8 minutes. If some team members are left unsatisfied with the time limit on the discussion, encourage them to elaborate their ideas in a follow-up email. By moving to each idea in turn with a fixed time limit, you can avoid getting caught up in minutiae and digressions.

Remember, some of your team members will excel during Step 5 and will want to explore the nuances of each idea. Conversely, others will find this detailed analysis tedious and boring. You want to strike a balance to ensure that the analytical folks have a chance to show off their stuff while moving quickly to get through all the ideas and keep your entire team engaged.

Recall that in the Ideation step (Step 3), I suggested that you ask participants to set aside their negative reactions to ideas. During the Logical Analysis step, you take the opportunity to revisit those negative reactions. Encourage those who have strong feelings about any idea to communicate their thoughts and feelings at this point.

In the time since team members had their first emotional reaction to an idea, the intensity of that reaction will have subsided. Anyone who had a strong negative reaction will now be in a better state to calmly explain it. I find that letting some time pass is an effective way to rationally explore the emotional reactions to ideas without letting those emotions rule the process.

After spending a few minutes on an idea, would you feel like you had done a proper analysis? Of course not! Often, the team will not have all the information necessary to adequately analyze each idea during the meeting. In order to perform a proper analysis, ask for volunteers. The biggest proponents and/or opponents of a given idea will usually be eager to collect any additional information the team feels it needs. If the need arises, I may call a separate meeting so the team can review the pros and cons of each idea to everyone's satisfaction.

At the end of Step 5, your problem-solving team will have a rich set of ideas with the pros and cons for each idea spelled out. The analytical folks on the team will have chimed in and provided the data and assessment that the team needs to move forward. You are now ready for Step 6, the Planning step, which I affectionately call "finding the path of least danger."

# Step 6: Planning

Enneagram Type 6 is at the core of the Head-Thinking-Anxiety center; as such, 6s will actively pursue minimizing their anxiety. Uncertainty and risk increase anxiety the most for Type 6s. Therefore, they naturally prepare for the future by planning ahead and seeking to minimize risk.

Type 6s can look at a number of scenarios and, using their anxiety level as a guide, instinctively spot the one with the fewest unknowns, the fewest pitfalls, and the highest likelihood of success. Using the pro/con analysis generated in Step 5, the 6 can assess each scenario and plot a path into the future to foresee likely outcomes. They can predict which ideas have the clearest path to the goal because those ideas cause the 6 the least amount of anxiety. This Type 6 dynamic comes into play in Step 6 of problem solving.

**Planning the Path of Least Danger**

## The Path of Least Danger

Having worked through the logical analysis of Step 5, the team will have reached a general consensus as to which ideas are the most viable and favorable for getting to the goal. This is the indication that your team has naturally arrived at Step 6, the Planning step. You can treat these favorable ideas as the framework for your solution—the skeleton, as it were. Now it is time to add the meat.

*If you fail to plan, you are planning to fail!*

In this step, the meat includes all the details associated with following the plan to achieve the goal. What resources are needed? How much do those resources cost? Who needs to be involved and when? What is the schedule for implementation? All these details need to be mapped out for presentation to the stakeholders responsible for allocating those resources. Enlisting the help of a team member with project management skills makes sense at this point in the process. It is exactly this skill set that comes into play in Step 6.

### Plan A/Plan B

At this point, you still may have a couple of viable paths to get to the goal. You may want to split your problem-solving team into smaller groups of advocates for each viable idea and let each group build a plan. As the details are fleshed out, you will see which idea has the shorter schedule, which has the lower cost, which requires the fewest people, and which has the fewest uncertainties and risks. With that knowledge, the team can develop a Plan A and a backup Plan B.

In Step 6, you will have decided the one or two ideas or sets of ideas that get you to the goal and solve the problem. You will have put together a detailed plan to implement the ideas. The team is now prepared to present the plan to the stakeholders and sponsors, especially those who can allocate the resources necessary to make the plan come true. Now is the time to promote the plan!

# Step 7: Promotion

Now that your team has identified the best path to the goal, your problem-solving team should be revved up and ready to charge down that path. However, the broader group of stakeholders will not yet be at the same excitement level. Now is the time to inspire that wider group—including the executive sponsors—to the same level of enthusiasm as the team. It is time for the team to sell the plan to all the stakeholders. It is time to tap the dynamic of Enneagram Type 7.

**Promoting the Plan**

## *Tapping into Your Inner Salesperson*

People in sales or political roles will understand this phase of problem solving well. A salesperson or politician must present a story with a bright future and receive permission to proceed and create that future for their customers or constituents. Step 7 of problem solving is similar.

When I facilitate problem-solving groups during Step 7, I recommend that the team create a presentation that tells a story. The first part of that story sets the stage: you remind your stakeholders of the pain they are experiencing because of their daunting problem. To make this more dramatic, let's call the problem *the dragon*. Then, you introduce your heroes—the team of highly credible and talented folks ready to face the dragon. You may want to share some examples of havoc wreaked by the dragon, and some stories of early, unsuccessful attempts to slay the dragon. Then, you will want to share your heroes' insight that exposed an alternative path to addressing the dragon problem. Finally, your story will explain the careful preparation the heroes have made to tame the dragon, thereby eliminating the problem once and for all. And there you stop.

What do you think that your executive sponsors/decision makers will do at this point? In my experience, having facilitated this process many times, the response is unequivocally "Go Get That Dragon!" I have found that all reasonable requests for resources—people, equipment, and cash—are made available for the dragon-taming quest. Also, there is a strong sense of empathy about the shared problem and anticipation of the beautiful world in which the dragon no longer terrorizes the citizens. That anticipation is infectious, and the executive sponsors will feel it. The broader organization will eagerly support your heroes in their quest too. That widespread support is important since taming this dragon will not be easy and will require everyone's cooperation.

I may have stretched the dragon metaphor to the limits here, but I think it does highlight the important step of having the team get explicit permission from the executive sponsors in order to proceed. This is similar to a sales process. I recommend that the team enlist the help of an enthusiastic, sales-oriented person to assist them in creating and telling a compelling story. Once your team has received permission to move forward, you arrive at Step 8, in which you act to solve the problem.

# Step 8: Implementation

Talk, talk, talk, talk, talk. That is all your team has been doing for the first seven steps. Enneagram Type 8s are not particularly fond of talking without taking action. Well, now is the time for action. Step

8 harnesses the dynamic of Enneagram Type 8. The team now has a plan in place and the project has the resources it needs, so this is the moment to move into action and execute the plan.

**Get Busy!**

Having gone through the process of developing and promoting the plan, most team members are eager to get into action by Step 8. The team now has envisioned a clear path to a successful outcome, and they will want to start down that path with enthusiasm and vigor.

The actual implementation will vary depending on the plan developed in Step 6. It could take weeks, months, or even years. Of all the steps in problem solving, Step 8 usually takes the longest. Successful implementation will take determination by your team, meaning moving forward daily towards the goal.

Referring back to the Enneagram diagram, Type 8 is connected to both Type 2 and Type 5. The Type 2 dynamic draws the team forward, keeping in mind the benefit that the stakeholders will enjoy upon successful completion of the project.

On the other hand, Type 5 is the analytical type, prone to paralysis by analysis. When the team encounters obstacles, there will be a tendency to fall back to Step 5, which is completely natural. The trick is to recognize this, move quickly through Steps 5, 6, and 7, and then back to action in Step 8. While the Type 8 dynamic dominates Step 8, the dynamics of the other types—particularly 5, 6, and 7—will be critical to keep the team moving forward and to prevent the project from stalling.

## Start Small, End Big

I have worked with teams that simply do not have a lot of natural Type 8 energy. If this happens with your team, try starting small and building on short-term successes; this is a great recipe for building and keeping up momentum towards the goal.

For instance, when implementing solutions that will affect a company's product development process, I advise my team to pick one smaller product development project and prototype the solutions with that development team.

By engaging with that one smaller team, you can learn what works and what doesn't. You can develop the materials you will need to communicate the solutions to other teams. And you can demonstrate the positive effects that the solutions have on outcomes. Recording and communicating these effects make it that much easier for each successive team to adopt the new solution. After a while, all the teams are using your new solution, mitigating the problems, and accomplishing the goals of your initiative.

## *Celebrate!*

Your team has achieved the goal and solved the problem! Now is the time for a well-deserved celebration. The team has taken a long journey through the eight steps. They are now feeling a combination of relief, exhaustion, and perhaps a bit of trepidation. Some may even be feeling shock due to the change that has transpired in the organization.

Inasmuch as most organizations and teams would like to think they are done with the initiative after the victory celebration, there is still one step left in the process. It will occur whether or not the team does it intentionally. Better outcomes result when the team takes Step 9 with intent.

# Step 9: Integration

Your problem-solving team has performed an apparent miracle. A transformative change has taken place within the organization. Results have been measured and confirmed. The team reached the goal they set out to achieve, and the problem has been solved. Is it time to move on?

Well, hold on just one minute. Whenever there is a transformative change within an organization, there will be perceived "winners" and "losers." There will be those whose positions in the company are apparently improved and those whose positions are perceived to be diminished. Humans are great at detecting these types of changes—we can't help ourselves; it's what we do.

Step 9 in the problem-solving process involves reaching out to all those people affected by the transformation and understanding what is and is not working well in the posttransformation organization. Enneagram Type 9 is called the Peacemaker. They tend to be empathetic and gifted at calming people who are in an agitated state. Step 9 leverages the dynamic of Enneagram Type 9.

**Integrating**

### Generous Listening

At this point in the problem-solving process, the most important skill is listening. It is particularly important to listen to those who have undergone disruptive change. Not only has this change been emotionally unsettling, there also may be unforeseen issues impeding their new workflows. It is important to capture these issues, address the concerns as well as possible, and ensure that all workflows are manageable.

### Continuous Improvement

During Step 9, someone may raise an issue of great magnitude and importance that requires more than a simple, quick fix. Note that the Enneagram diagram is depicted as a circle, implying that the

Enneagram-based problem-solving process is circular rather than linear; there is a reason Step 1 follows Step 9. After a transformative change in Step 8, new problems identified during Step 9 can be addressed with the same process. In this manner, an organization can continually evaluate its effectiveness and take steps to ameliorate problems in a never-ending cycle of continuous improvement.

## Problems with Problem Solving

I once shared the concepts of Enneagram-based problem solving with a group of university students. After the talk, one student explained how she was working in environmental studies and policy and that the process they used to work through different policy proposals was continually getting stuck. She also observed that the process did not include some of the steps that the Enneagram-based problem-solving approach includes, specifically Steps 2 and 7, in which the team reaches out to the broader group of stakeholders. She realized after my talk that it was precisely because her team was skipping these steps that her initiatives became stuck.

There are many different approaches to problem solving. You can find dozens if not hundreds of methods and books on the subject. They all follow more or less the same pattern as the Enneagram-based approach—after all, we are all humans trying to solve problems.

The curious thing I notice when I compare a given problem-solving process to the Enneagram-based approach is that some process steps are skipped and some are overemphasized. The Enneagram-based approach has nine steps. Other approaches may have fewer than nine or more than nine. Interestingly, the biases in an author's problem-solving process compared to the Enneagram method will often reveal the author's Enneagram type!

For instance, if Type 5s develop a problem-solving process, they may only include a few steps: define the problem, analyze solutions, implement. Often, they will include several analysis steps since they want to play to their own strengths: perform root cause analysis, analyze several approaches, develop a cost-benefit analysis of each approach, etc. Their process may dwell on steps that are the 5's forte before finally moving on to a subsequent step. Also, a process developed by a Type 5 may exclude steps that require reaching out to stakeholders, developing a committed team, and considering people's emotional reactions. We humans tend to downplay our weaknesses and play up our strengths. (In the case of Type 5, a weakness and a strength are "reaching out to others" and "analyzing data," respectively.)

On the other hand, the Enneagram-based approach takes into account each Enneagram type and explicitly includes and leverages the strengths of each. This makes solutions more resilient and sustainable. Environmental policy development is a great example of a complex challenge that would benefit from the Enneagram-based approach because of the diversity of stakeholders and possible solutions.

# Get Started

When I conducted my first problem-solving initiative at Palm, I simply followed the process I outlined in this chapter. The Enneagram-based approach focused team members on our common problems—the dragons—and motivated us to work together to solve those common problems. Together we tamed many dragons.

There may be a dragon that you want your team to tame. By all means, get started! If you systematically follow the steps in this chapter, I anticipate that you will realize similar success in achieving your goals.

## *Problems Everywhere*

The numbers on the Enneagram reveal the numerical order of the steps in which humans naturally solve problems. The Enneagram provides a framework for teams to work together collectively and collaboratively to tackle large challenges. Since teams are comprised of individuals, each with his or her own Enneagram type, understanding the types of the individuals on your team will reveal how effectively your team can move through the entire problem-solving process.

Each time I use this process, I gain additional insights into the dynamics of teams: shared leadership; the relationships between Enneagram type and creativity and between type and time; and which types work well together and why. I share these insights in the following chapters. They will explain the dynamics of your particular team and help you accelerate the team based on their strengths. Also, you will find tips on how to fill in the gaps to overcome any weaknesses.

In the next chapter (Chapter 3, "Shared Leadership"), we will explore how to leverage the dynamics of each Enneagram type and each team member to maintain momentum as you move your team through the problem-solving process.

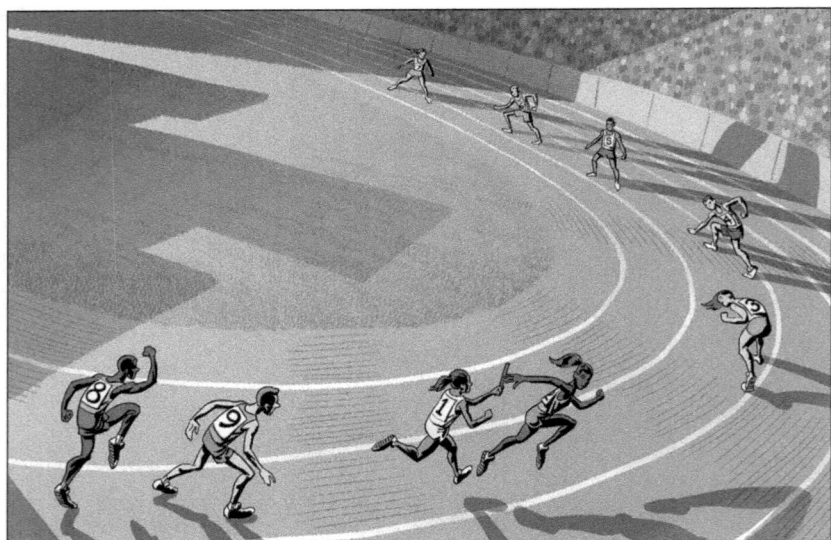

# CHAPTER 3

# Shared Leadership

P eople naturally play to their strengths. Left unconstrained, the 8s jump into action, the 1s argue with the 8s about the *right* thing to do, the 3s and the 7s chime in with more ideas, 2s offer to help the 8s, the 6s forecast doom, the 5s silently watch and amuse themselves, the 4s relish the drama, and the 9s quietly leave the room.

The Enneagram problem-solving framework provides an organizing principle that transforms a group of individual actors into a coherent working team. It highlights how each Enneagram dynamic contributes to problem solving and how team members with the corresponding type can take a lead when a project requires that dynamic. The most effective teams value these style differences and encourage team members to share leadership throughout the problem-solving process.

In *First, Break All the Rules*, Marcus Buckingham and Curt Coffman use the metaphor of a bumpy, two-lane highway versus a ten-lane superhighway to highlight our differences in capabilities. When we are young, especially in the US, we are taught that we can achieve anything we want if we try hard enough. But, as we mature, we realize that this belief—like Santa Claus, the Easter Bunny, and the Tooth

Fairy—is a myth. Intuitively, we understand that each of us is unique with a distinct set of capabilities, strengths, and weaknesses, and that many of these capabilities are inherent—nature, not nurture.

Buckingham and Coffman go on to say that the myth that anyone can do anything is one of the "rules" you need to break in order to build effective teams and organizations. I was a hiring manager when I read that book and, based on my experience, I couldn't have agreed more. I was left wondering how I could identify a person's built-in superhighway during an interview before having worked with them.

# Nine Superhighways

The Enneagram answered that question for me. As I studied the Enneagram types, I came to understand the built-in superhighway capabilities of each type. When I was interviewing candidates, I now had a tool that could help me answer key questions: Is this person detail oriented or focused on the big picture? Does this person need to work with others on a team or can they work solo for long stretches? Will this person challenge others and their assumptions or will they go with the flow? Does this person like to plan things out or shoot first and ask questions later? These insights can be tremendously helpful in finding the best candidate for the job.

---

## My Favorite Interview Question

---

I have discovered an interview question that will reveal a candidate's Enneagram type: "Describe your problem-solving process."

I say nothing more and let them start talking. Most people will start strong and then stumble at some point. For instance, most will say that you start by defining the problem. Then you need to come up with an idea, and so on. As the candidate talks, listen carefully to each step they describe, noting which steps they skip and which they overemphasize.

We all want to play to our strengths and downplay our weaknesses, especially in an interview. When they get to the step in the problem-solving process that corresponds to their own Enneagram type, most people will elaborate on that particular step, breaking it down into great detail. Then, when they move on from that step—if they move on at all—they describe the remaining steps dismissively.

My favorite answer was from a candidate who said, "First you understand the problem, then you research that problem, then you do root cause analysis on the problem." After describing those three steps the candidate stopped, looked up at me, and realized he'd forgotten one important thing. "And then you solve the problem."

Any guess what type this person is? This would be a classic answer for Type 1 with an intense focus on Step 1, defining the problem. After elaborating on Step 1, this candidate combined the remaining eight steps into one.

You can use the problem-solving framework described in the previous chapter (Chapter 2, "Problem Solving with the Enneagram") to assess a candidate's answer. Which steps did your candidates talk about at length? Which did they dismiss? The steps a candidate dwells on are strong candidates for their Enneagram type and show which parts of problem solving the candidate will be most interested in pursuing on the job.

The most remarkable thing I find is that many people never even bother to describe Step 8 (Implementation). After they finish speaking, I will mention that they have not described *solving* the problem, which will spur them to move on and describe additional steps, including Step 8.

One time, a candidate answered carefully and thoughtfully, describing each of the nine steps in the problem-solving process. I was stunned—it was the first and only time that has happened. It was not obvious to me what Enneagram type he was, but I was so impressed with the answer that I hired the candidate, and he was outstanding.

---

# Nature versus Nurture

Although the Enneagram can be instructive in determining one's own nature, it will not necessarily be helpful in predicting interest level for a particular job. For interest level, you can look at other indications, such as level of enthusiasm and prior work experiences. Also, you can speak with their references to learn whether or not the candidate loved doing that work.

However, even if someone loves some particular work, they may not have a ten-lane superhighway for that work. I love playing guitar, but that doesn't mean I am very good—just ask my family! The ideal candidate not only loves what they do, they also have the Enneagram type that delivers the ten-lane superhighway for the job.

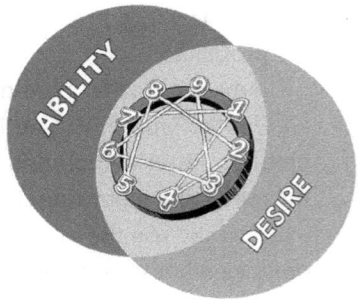

# Balanced Problem Solving

As a manager, you would like to have a team with a diverse set of capabilities, so that when your team faces a challenge you can draw on the relevant strengths to address that challenge. Likewise, as you move a team through the problem-solving process, you will find that different strengths come into play at each step. Having a team with diverse Enneagram types will allow those types with the relevant strengths to make extraordinary contributions.

Ideally, one of your team members will have both the interest and the superhighway capabilities for each step in problem solving and will provide leadership during that step. As you complete one step of the process and move on to the next, a new leader with the appropriate skills and interest can emerge. Leadership transition can happen naturally, even unconsciously. As a facilitator, your job is simply to ensure that the baton is passed smoothly and in a timely manner.

# Movements in the Enneagram

We have discussed how the behaviors of each Enneagram type can change over time. Enneagram types can move along their paths of integration or disintegration and behave like other types, depending on whether they are in a secure or an insecure state.

In Chapter 2, "Problem Solving with the Enneagram," we explored how problem solving follows clockwise movement around the Enneagram, starting with Step 1 and following the nine sequential steps around the circle.

Individual types can also access the dynamics of the types in either the clockwise or counterclockwise direction. However, the dynamics of the type in the clockwise direction from their own can be some of the most difficult behaviors for individuals to access. In other words, the hardest behaviors for any Enneagram type to emulate are those that come naturally to the next Enneagram type in the clockwise direction. With the exception of the 9-to-1 transition, that is the Enneagram type with the next higher number.

This means that if you are working on the problem-solving step that corresponds to your Enneagram type, then the most difficult set

of behaviors for you to emulate are those in the next step. This concept applies to teams as well: a team overweight with a type corresponding to any one step will want to stay on that step, playing to their collective strength. They may resist moving to the next, more challenging step. Based on this understanding of the Enneagram, you can appreciate how easy it is for a team to get stuck.

How do we overcome this difficulty? Shared leadership is one answer. Passing the leadership baton from step to step with full team awareness and support accomplishes three important things: 1) it overcomes the difficulty of clockwise movement around the Enneagram; 2) it demonstrates team progress, moving from one step to the next; and 3) it brings new, enthusiastic leadership energy to each step in the process.

In the following sections, I describe: (1) the leadership skills of each Enneagram type that come into play during the corresponding step in problem solving; (2) the other types that can naturally access the relevant strengths; and (3) the types needing to restrain energy that could be counterproductive during the step. Bear in mind how the leadership styles change from step to step and how important it is to facilitate these transitions during problem solving.

# Step 1 Leadership: Problem-Goal

As the internal anger type, Enneagram Type 1s have an inner critical voice that guides their strong sense of right and wrong. They are alert to problems, and their inner voice persistently reminds them of what should and shouldn't be. This internal critic drives 1s to examine a problem in excruciating detail and provides a clear vision of what the world should look like once the problem is solved.

Type 1 is the ideal type for leading Step 1, in which the team defines the problem. The 1s persist in examining a problem until it is completely understood. Once the problem description is complete, they can then turn to envisioning the beautiful world in which the problem is eliminated. This vision serves as the destination for the team—the goal for the problem-solving effort.

**Other Types.** The wings of Type 1—Type 9 and Type 2—may share Type 1's strong sense of right and wrong. These types can be great contributors, and possibly leaders, in Step 1. Type 4 has a path of integration to the 1, so a secure 4 is another candidate for leadership in this step. Type 6s like to think through everything that can go wrong, so they can be good at describing problems. Type 7s are connected to the 1's energy through their path of disintegration. The 7s can sense what will cause others displeasure; if they can comfortably tap into that sense, they can serve as leaders in this step. They can also excel at defining the goal—the pleasing world in which the problem is solved and everyone is happy again.

**Energies to Rein In.** The 3, the 5, and the 8 may have more challenges in Step 1. The 3s will have ideas for solving the problem before the problem is well defined. They tend to move the conversation to solutions, disrupting the conversation about the problem itself. Those with Type 3 energy can be encouraged to write down their ideas, so you can return to them in Step 3.

Those with Type 5 energy may have trouble speaking up and expressing their perspective on the problem and their vision for the goals. The 5 needs to be reassured that there are no incorrect perspectives on describing the problem and that everyone's perspective is equally valid. The leader in this phase needs to ensure that all team members contribute, even if they are reluctant to share.

Finally, the 8s will likely be rolling their eyes during this step. While 8s are good at detecting weaknesses and can leverage that skill to define the problem, they will also be eager to jump into action. Step

1 is definitely not the time for action. The 8s will have to check their inclination to act and instead focus on defining the problem and creating a shared vision for the future.

## The Type 8 CEO

I am often hired by Type 8 CEOs serving as the executive sponsor for a problem-solving initiative. Typically, 8s do not see themselves as part of the problem, which can bias their problem assessments. They are predisposed to think that challenges come from external forces, not something they're doing.

If a team reveals to me that the CEO's behaviors are indeed part of the problem, I record the specific issues that are blocking the team without personifying the issues. I also coach the Type 8 CEO that the team may request some workflow changes that will touch on how the CEO interacts with the team. This coaching is usually enough to open up the CEO to the idea of making personal adjustments that will help the team overcome the challenges and resolve festering problems.

During Step 1, Type 1 CEOs look at problems much more critically and objectively, basing their assessment on their understanding of right and wrong, irrespective of their own self-interest. Type 1s are already critical of themselves, so if they see themselves as part of the problem they are perfectly willing to accept that.

# Step 2 Leadership: Stakeholder Identification

Being the external emotion type, Enneagram Type 2 energy is focused on helping others. During Step 2 in problem solving, the 2 will know instinctively who will benefit from a successful outcome of the problem-solving venture. The people involved in that venture, both actors and beneficiaries, are collectively the stakeholders in the project. Type 2s can build emotional bonds with the stakeholders, connecting them emotionally and viscerally to the project. The 2 is the ideal person to take the lead during this phase of the project and build the relationships necessary for the ultimate success of the problem-solving initiative.

**Other Types.** Sheer enthusiasm for the endeavor is another technique for building a team. This approach may not have the emotional sticking power that the 2 would bring, but it can be effective during the "honeymoon" phase of a project. Type 7s typically have a large network of relationships they can tap into. Their enthusiasm is infectious and helps build the cohesiveness necessary to move the effort forward. Like the 7, both Types 3 and 8—if they are on board with the goals defined in Step 1—can bring a sense of optimism that will motivate people to join the project.

**Energies to Rein In.** Step 2 is broad and inclusive. There is no type that would need to be reined in unless the individual had a propensity to exclude stakeholders or limit their participation. Step 2 is the time for inclusion, not exclusion. Types 1 and 6 can both be critical and judgmental, which can be exclusionary. Also, an 8 who is feeling threatened by the initiative may be critical of the venture. Since Step 2 is not the time for critical or judgmental thinking, those energies should be reined in.

## Who Is Your Best Friend?

During a workshop where people of all Enneagram types were present, I asked each participant to think about their best friends, especially during their high school years, and guess which Enneagram types they were. The primary pattern that emerged was that most people had best friends that were their same type. As the saying goes, "Birds of a feather flock together."

There were two notable exceptions. While most people said that their best friend was typically their own number, almost everyone mentioned that they had at some point a best friend who was a Type 7. Clearly, people like to be around the positive, enthusiastic, talkative, outgoing person who is the 7.

The other exception we discovered is that Type 2s could not pin down the type for their typical best friend. The 2s recalled being friends with all different types and no one type in particular. Type 2s are not motivated to be around those similar to themselves. They are motivated to be around people who will appreciate them and form an emotional bond with them. The 2's gift is their ability to have this relationship with any type. In fact, the hardest type to help—and receive appreciation from—would likely be another 2; they would just compete to outdo one another for appreciation, which would likely not end well.

When you are in Step 2, the 2 will be able to build relationships inclusively with all the other types, helping you to build a well-rounded team. The 7's network of relationships built on having fun together can also be used to recruit an enthusiastic team.

# Step 3 Leadership: Ideation

As the suppressed emotion type, Enneagram Type 3s have the remarkable gift of being able to generate fresh ideas without feeling constrained by emotional baggage. They can think freely, unencumbered, and will enthusiastically generate ideas with the aim of successfully solving the problem.

In Step 3, the leader must solicit ideas from all team members and stakeholders and, most importantly, not *react* to those ideas. The aim is to collect as many ideas as possible for later analysis. Type 3s would be ideal leaders for this part of the project since they provide both enthusiasm for successful outcomes and restraint from emotional reactions to any of the ideas.

**Other Types.** The most important leadership aspect in this step is impartial facilitation. After careful coaching, I have seen nearly every type perform well in this role—even I can do it as a Type 6! The three key requirements are to encourage the team, ensure that everyone contributes, and refrain from promoting your own ideas.

Type 3 has the magic combination of these three requirements. The other types that bring enthusiasm are the 7 and the 8. The types that make sure that others are heard are the 2, 4, 5, 6, and 9.

You can imagine that, other than the 3s, the enthusiastic types may be inclined to dominate the conversation. They need to be coached to ensure that they allow everyone a chance to chime in with ideas. Most importantly, the leader in this step needs to ensure that everyone expresses their ideas without fear of criticism. During Step 3, Type 1 is a special case, which I discuss next.

**Energies to Rein In.** The 1, 4, 6, and the critical 8 energies need to be checked during Step 3. In the Ideation phase, Type 1 has a curious tendency to want to revisit the problem descriptions. Certainly, if a new problem is aired, be sure to note that down. However, if the group returns to discussing problems already recorded, then the discussion must be redirected back to ideation. If you know you have Type 1s on your team who tend to rehash problems, it would be a good idea to coach them that the ideation meeting is future oriented, aiming to generate new ideas. Also, Type 1s have a strong sense of right and wrong, which can come into play as others share their ideas. Step 3 is not the time to be critical of ideas, so negative reactions and comments need to be suppressed at this point.

Other types that can have strong negative reactions to ideas are the 4, the 6, and the 8. The best way I have learned to minimize the vocalization of negative comments and keep a positive tone during Step 3 is to use the "Yes, and ..." technique described in Chapter 2, "Problem Solving with the Enneagram."

# Step 4 Leadership: Emotional Reaction

While every Enneagram type can have an emotional reaction to an idea, the internal emotion Type 4 is highly attuned to the emotional content in any idea. In Step 3 (Ideation), it was important to hold back negative reactions in order to generate the richest possible set of ideas. In Step 4, it is important to review and reflect on how people reacted to the ideas, both positively and negatively.

While some initiatives can combine Steps 3 and 4 as described in the previous chapter, for projects that must carefully consider the possible emotional reactions of all stakeholders, I dedicate time to this analysis. Type 4s are ideal for leading this discussion since they will have the most nuanced appreciation of others' reactions and a sense of what stakeholders will like. While many of us would like to think we are driven by logic and data, the truth is that emotions play an even greater role in our decision making. The ability to understand emotional reactions is critical for determining both the short- and long-term acceptability of any idea.

**Other Types.** All of us can have strong reactions to ideas. The point of Step 4 in problem solving is to appreciate your emotional reactions to ideas as well as the reactions of others. The leader of this discussion does not necessarily have to have the same nuanced understanding of emotional response as Type 4 but must appreciate and discern varying degrees of emotional reactions, both positive and negative.

The two wings of the 4—Types 3 and 5—are both excellent observers of people and capable of discerning other team members' emotional reactions. The 2's desire to help others gives them insight into how people are reacting emotionally. The 6 and the 9 have strong anxiety and anger sensors, respectively; the 6 will know if there is danger of emotional pushback on an idea, and the 9 will sense if an idea could cause discord and confrontation. On the other hand, the 7 will get a sense of how positively an idea is viewed and will be drawn towards those positive emotional reactions.

**Energies to Rein In.** The 1 and 8 may have more difficulty reflecting on emotional reactions. The 8 can be impatient—exploring feelings and emotions may seem like a waste of time to them. The 1's own sense of right and wrong may overwhelm their appreciation of others' emotional reactions to ideas.

# Step 5 Leadership: Logical Analysis

As the internal anxiety type, Enneagram Type 5's anxious energy conveys an extraordinary ability to collect and comb through mountains of data. Type 5s will follow the data wherever it takes them and will not be satisfied until they believe they have exhausted all avenues. At Step 5, your team will have developed a handful of promising ideas that need careful consideration. Type 5 is ideally suited to take up the leadership mantle in this step and guide the team through the pro/con analysis of each idea.

A special trait of the 5s is their unbiased pursuit of information. They would just as soon collect all available data and not leave anything out. Other types tend to have biases that cause them to filter out certain data. While those filters may help them arrive at a decision more quickly, they might overlook important information that the 5 would have uncovered.

## Decision Tree Diagrams

I once had the pleasure of working for a Type 5. At our weekly one-on-one meeting, he would share an analysis that he had done in the preceding week. Regardless of the topic—be it a new direction for funding the company or a decision to explore new product ideas—he would create an elaborate decision tree diagram, laying out all the options. We used those diagrams as the basis of our conversation. This experience gave me insight into the way that 5s collect, organize, and present information.

**Other Types.** Type 1s can also carefully collect and analyze data. They are compelled to collect all data relevant to an issue at hand in the pursuit of understanding that issue perfectly. The 6 is comfortable in this role too, though based on my personal experience I suspect that Type 6s are better at collecting data when anxiety levels are lower and analyzing data when anxiety levels are higher.

Both the 1 and 6 tend to have strong filters that make them prone to overlooking data that the 5 may not, so these two types need to keep that in mind, using the broader perspectives of all team members to ensure that nothing is overlooked.

Another natural data collector is Type 7, though their method is slightly different. Unlike the solitary data collection typical of the 5, Type 7s tend to collect data through their interactions with others. For analysis of that data, the secure 7 has access to quiet contemplation as they move along their path of integration. In their integrated state, they can calmly comb through and analyze the collected data in the same manner as Type 5.

Type 8s are connected to Type 5 along their path of disintegration. The 8s can excel at collecting and analyzing data and tend to exhibit this behavior when they feel that their security is being threatened. If they can channel those capabilities even in their secure state, they can be great leaders in this phase.

**Energies to Rein In.** Clearly, Step 5 is not the step to rush into action. Many types will want to do that, including the 8, the 3, the 2, the 7, and the anxious 6. To avoid rushing this step, those with the energy to jump into action need to redirect those inclinations. Step 5 is a good time for building small prototypes and testing assumptions. Those with the propensity for action can contribute to those action-oriented tasks that still fall into the realm of collecting and analyzing data.

# Step 6 Leadership: Planning

The active Type 6 mind continuously connects dots into the future. As the suppressed anxiety type, they seek to minimize their feelings of anxiety by identifying a path to the goal that has a high likelihood for success. As 6s review the pro/con analysis of each idea in Step 5, they can intuitively assign probabilities to outcomes, which gives them insight into the most promising ideas.

The 6s are driven by the fear of failure and the danger that failure represents, so they can easily identify the danger in each option. Their gift is being able to identify the path of least danger. In their minds, the 6s connect the dots along the path to the goal for each idea. The path with the clearest set of dots stands out starkly to them. This makes the 6 well equipped to lead the group in both selecting the most promising ideas and creating a plan of action that connects the dots and guides the team to the desired goal.

The aphorism, "Failing to plan is planning to fail," captures the mindset of Type 6. In Step 6, you plan schedules, budgets, resource allocation, and contingencies that will withstand scrutiny from the stakeholders. Before further investment in the project, the action plan needs to be organized in a logical and palatable manner.

**Other Types.** The flip side of the fear of failure is the desire to succeed. Approaching Step 6 from that angle, the 3 can also envision the steps that lead to successful outcomes. Type 7 has a similar capability. Both of these types have less patience for planning than Type 6, so they may have a tendency to shortcut the planning process. The devil is in the details, and Type 6 is attuned to rooting out that scary devil. Other types need to keep that in mind as they develop a detailed plan. One approach to doing this is to keep asking, "What if?" That question is on a continuous loop in the minds of the 6s and drives them to think through all the possibilities and contingencies.

Types 9 and 5 can also lead in this phase. While they are less guided internally by a sense of failure or success, they both have the ability to read the team's reactions and patiently think through the steps to a successful outcome. The 5 will be driven by not wanting to appear foolish, and the 9 will be driven by the desire to avoid conflict. Either motivation is sufficient to drive the creation of a viable, detailed plan.

**Energies to Rein In.** Type 8s want to act first and ask questions later. Step 6 is exactly the time for asking questions, not the time for jumping into action. On the other hand, there is no such thing as a perfect project plan. While Type 1s can be excellent at thinking through the steps to a successful outcome, they also tend to overplan and lose flexibility. These tendencies need to be checked.

Finally, planning is a cerebral activity, well suited for the logical thinking prevalent in the thinking center but less suited for the emotional thinking prevalent in the feeling center. While Type 3s suppress emotion, Types 2 and 4 in the feeling center generally do not, and they need to be aware of that tendency during the Planning phase. The focus of Step 6 is on the step-by-step details and the practical nuts and bolts of the plan.

# Step 7 Leadership: Promotion

The external anxiety Type 7 is motivated to create a positive environment and build enthusiasm for the next adventure. This motivation drives them to encourage and embolden the project stakeholders in Step 7, making them perfectly tuned for leadership during this step. The 7's dynamic is invaluable for helping the team coalesce the broader group of stakeholders around the plan and getting the buy-in, endorsements, sponsorships, budget allocations, and so on necessary to execute the plan.

The 7's natural ability in this role is evidenced by the fact that many of our elected politicians are 7s. The kind of leadership that gets a politician elected is exactly the sort of leadership required by the project team in Step 7. The 7 can lead the team to create the "pitch deck" presentation for the project, deliver that pitch, and navigate the nuances of the stakeholder communication to get the support the team needs to move the project towards implementation.

In a nutshell, the key activity in Step 7 is instilling trust and confidence in the sponsors and stakeholders that the team will accomplish the plan, meet the goals, and solve the problem. Type 7s are masters at instilling trust in others.

**Other Types.** The 3 can also serve in the leadership role in Step 7. Type 3s can pitch the project in an enthusiastic, positive light and will know how to present what success looks like in the completed project. They will be attuned to the broader group's reactions to the plan and adept at making adjustments on the fly to get the endorsement to move forward.

The 8 can also pitch the project. Their desire to start implementing the solution will convey enthusiasm, as long as it is not seen as exasperation. The 8 exudes confidence, and that confidence will embolden the stakeholders to support the project. The 8's direct style will come off as sincere. If most of the stakeholders are 8s, that style will resonate with them, allowing the 8 to build rapport and trust. If you expect that there may be a nay-saying 8 among the stakeholders, then having an 8 on your team give the pitch will provide a counterbalance to that negative energy.

Type 2s can also be great at making pitches. The 2 will highlight all the benefits of the project to the stakeholders and show how much it will help them. The 2 will have developed the relationships with the stakeholders on which the team can rely to get support for the project.

The leadership styles of Type 4 and Type 9 can also be effective in Step 7. The 4 approach will portray the positive impact of the project on the organization. If the stakeholders are empathetic types, then this style can be effective. The 4 can read the audience's emotional reactions and respond accordingly to sway the conversation. The 9 will also show how the project will improve the organization. The quiet confidence of the 9 can reassure the sponsors and stakeholders and give them the courage to move forward.

**Energies to Rein In.** While the team needs to be able to address questions from stakeholders regarding contingency plans, Step 7 is not typically the time to dwell on negative issues. Therefore, it is best to avoid the self-critical energy of Type 1 in this step. Furthermore, Step 7 is not the time for the indecisiveness common to Type 5 and the doubtfulness typical of Type 6. The team should present a determined, unified front to the stakeholders.

Types 1, 5, and 6 can serve as leaders in this step, but they will have to restrain their natural tendencies in order to get the endorsement of the stakeholders. Conversely, if most of the stakeholders are Type 1, 5, or 6, then it may be best to have a presenter with that same Enneagram type. Similar types naturally have higher levels of rapport and trust, and that trust will influence their perception of the project as a whole.

# Step 8 Leadership: Implementation

The external anger Type 8 wants to get started, and Step 8 is the point in problem solving where action-oriented leadership shines. With the plan in place and the resources allocated, the 8 can direct the team in executing that plan. The strength and confidence of Type 8s inspire and motivate others to follow their lead. Type 8s are not afraid to fail. If they go down a path that proves to be unproductive, they are quick to course-correct and try something new. There is little fretting or pondering; the dynamic in Step 8 is action, which the Type 8 leader delivers.

Since other types are more susceptible to a fear of failure, Type 8 in particular provides the confidence to help others overcome their inhibitions and take action. If feelings are hurt along the way, that is a price that must be paid to achieve the goal. Conflicts will arise in this step, and 8s tap into their anger-based energy and easily rise to the challenge. They can get beyond a confrontation and move on to the task at hand. They won't let feelings get in the way of getting the job done. They tend not to take things personally, and they expect others not to either.

**Other Types.** While no other type has the 8's capacity for directing action, most types can lead during this step with their own distinct style. Type 2s can rely on their emotional connections and relationships to lead the team to action. Valuable leadership assets in this phase are the 3's persistent pursuit of success and endless energy. The secure 5 can behave like Type 8 during the Implementation phase. Type 6 can suppress their anxiety and use their intimate knowledge of the project plan to guide the team. The enthusiasm of the 7 can inspire the team to action as can the quiet confidence of the 9.

**Energies to Rein In.** Issues will occur during the Implementation phase that can disrupt the flow of the project. It is important to address these issues quickly in order to prevent the project from veering off course and not recovering. Leadership styles represented by Types 1, 5, and 6 may spend too much time dwelling on these issues. When an issue does surface, it is important to overcome it quickly without overanalyzing it.

Additionally, Type 6s will have to exhibit flexibility and not stick too rigidly to the plan. Types 7 and 9 will have to avoid shying away from confrontation when it arises. The 7 can also be distracted from the main job at hand and will have to resist that temptation. Type 1 will have to compromise on the desire for perfection, embracing the idea that the perfect is the enemy of the good. Type 4 will be most susceptible to getting wrapped up in other people's feelings during this phase, which could slow progress. The 2s will also be sensitive to feelings but will likely not let that sensitivity get in the way of progress since they can move to the dynamic of Type 8s along their path of disintegration. When the going gets tough on the project and success becomes doubtful, the 3s will have to resist their fear of failure and their temptation to give up.

# Step 9 Leadership: Integration

The project is complete and the goal has been accomplished. Yet, there still may be a sense of discord in the air as people adjust to the new environment. The main project team is withdrawing, along with the Type 8 energy that drove the team. This is when the suppressed anger Type 9 leadership needs to emerge, with the ability to understand the issues that have left people unsettled and to facilitate harmony in the new environment. The 9s are highly attuned to sensing anger and the potential for conflict. If they sense this, the 9 will immediately engage to mitigate possible conflict. Type 9s tend to stay calm even as others are emotionally activated and agitated. Their calmness has a settling effect on those around them that brings people back into a conversation that leads to conflict resolution.

**Other Types.** The critical factor to Step 9 in problem solving is creating an environment for listening, empathy, and dialogue. It is not the time for reacting, jumping to conclusions, or taking action. While the 9 encapsulates this energy perfectly, other types can also serve well in this role.

Type 1 will listen intently for any problems. The feeling types can all be attentive listeners: Type 2s will listen to determine how they can help. Type 3s will listen to determine whether the project was considered a success or a failure. The 4s will sense the emotions of the speaker. The thinking types—Types 5, 6, and 7—are compelled to listen in order to create a calm environment that will lower their anxiety. The 7s will listen to find a way to make people happy, especially in how others see them. The 6s will listen to find a path to reduce any chaos or confusion that is causing anxiety. The integrated 6 can look much like a 9 in this capacity. The 5s, as always, will be collecting information they can use to make themselves feel safer.

**Energies to Rein In.** Clearly, this is not a time for more confrontation. This is the time to smooth ruffled feathers. The confrontational style of the 8 will not be helpful in this phase. Any type that has moved into a reactive state, along their path of disintegration, will likely only aggravate the situation. On the other hand, moving along the path of integration into a state that is not emotionally charged can create emotional distance from the issues. That distance would allow the listening leader to assess the situation objectively.

# Passing the Baton

Each Enneagram type is optimized for a specific step in problem solving. The dynamics of each type are exactly those needed at the corresponding step in the Enneagram-based problem-solving process. The fact that a different leadership style is required for each step highlights the benefits of sharing leadership responsibilities during a problem-solving initiative.

Recall that among the hardest behaviors for each Enneagram type to emulate are those of the next type in the clockwise direction around the Enneagram circle. Rather than tackling a difficult problem-solving step, each type will have a tendency to play to its strength and stay in the step that requires their specific talents. That tendency makes it easy for both individuals and teams to get stuck in the problem-solving sequence.

Shared leadership—allowing new leaders to emerge at each successive step of the problem-solving process—relieves the current leader and provides new and appropriate energy for the next step. This is a great way to keep the team from getting stuck.

Knowing which leadership styles are appropriate in each step allows all types to tap into their own talents and bring their relevant styles to bear at the appropriate step the in problem-solving sequence.

The leadership baton can be passed consciously or unconsciously among team members. If you're facilitating the process and moving your team through the steps, you may notice that new leadership emerges organically at each step. If the team struggles, you can encourage emergent leaders to share their unique talents during the next step of problem solving.

In Chapter 4, "The Leadership Path of Growth," we will explore how each of us can use the Enneagram to find a path in our own personal journey to develop our leadership skills and access the leadership styles of all the Enneagram types.

# The Leadership Path of Growth

I have always wanted a personal coach. I know a number of personal coaches, and I notice that many of them are Type 7, which makes perfect sense. The 7's ebullience is infectious and inspirational—at least to everyone other than a Type 6 like me.

Unabashed optimism can seem inauthentic to the 6. I knew instinctively that I would always be questioning the approach of the 7, and that constant questioning would likely frustrate a Type 7 coach. If I allowed myself to be myself in that relationship it would be a train wreck, but being my authentic self seemed like the bare minimum for working with a personal coach. What to do?

The Enneagram gave me the answer. My path of personal growth lies mainly on my path of integration, which for the 6 points to Type 9. What better personal coach for a 6 than a 9, whose very nature models the behaviors to which I aspire?

I did hire a coach who is a 9. She is empathetic and understands my Type 6 angst. She also illuminates the 9 perspective for me and shows me how to appreciate that perspective along my path of integration. As I open myself to that perspective, I am able to appreciate many different perspectives, much like the typical 9 would. Having a coach of the type along my path of integration has been an enlightening experience.

# Access to New Behaviors

As a leader, it is important to understand and appreciate each of the nine Enneagram dynamics as well as improve your ability to emulate any dynamic. When a situation calls for a particular dynamic, as we saw in the sequence of problem solving, you want to have access that dynamic.

Each type has greater or lesser difficulty accessing the other dynamics. As each type moves into the secure state along their path of integration, it becomes easier to access any of the other dynamics. This chapter describes the movement along the path of integration—represented by the direction of the arrows in the diagram—for each Enneagram type and explores how even the most challenging dynamics become accessible.

**Enneagram Paths of Integration**

Recall that for most types, the most difficult dynamic to access is the next type in the clockwise direction around the Enneagram circle. In the following sections, I will illustrate how you can emulate that dynamic by moving along your path of integration.

# Another Word on Wings

Readers familiar with Enneagram wing types may be puzzled by my assertion that the behaviors associated with the next higher type can be among the least accessible for any given type. After all, the next higher (clockwise) type is one of the wings of that type, and wing types represent accessible behaviors, right? For instance, wouldn't a Type 1 with a Type 2 wing have access to the 2's behaviors?

I will admit that a person whose wing is the next higher type will likely have an easier time emulating those behaviors than someone whose wing is the next lower type. But a person able to emulate *some* of the behaviors of the next higher type may not have access to *all* the behaviors necessary for the next step in the problem-solving sequence. Also, if you feel that you have a strong wing in the next higher type, you may be accessing those behaviors because you have moved along your path of integration and are accessing those behaviors through your integrated type. In other words, Type 1 can access their wing Type 2 behaviors through their integrated Type 7.

# Path of Growth for Type 1 Leaders

For Type 1, the hardest behaviors to emulate are those typical of Type 2. Type 1 is the internal anger type of the Gut-Intuitive-Anger center, while Type 2 is the external emotion type of the Heart-Feeling-Emotion center. Not being in the feeling center, Type 1s place much less importance on feelings and emotional connections, especially when compared with the 2s.

**The Obstacle.** For the 1s, the highest priority is "getting it right." This priority creates a blind spot for the 1s; unlike 2s, Type 1s have trouble putting people ahead of their principles. They are driven by the critical inner voice telling them what is right and what is wrong. This inner voice overwhelms any appreciation for how others are feeling or how they may need to build emotional bonds with others to help them right the wrong they perceive. Because the most challenging behavior for the 1 is prioritizing emotional connections with others over their principles, they struggle with behaviors that come naturally to the 2.

**The Way Around: Integrate to Type 7.** As the 1s learn to quiet their inner critic and let go of their compulsion to get things perfect, they move along their path of integration towards the fun-seeking Type 7. The 7-like enthusiastic behaviors are contagious and allow the 1s to build emotional connections to stakeholders who help them in their mission.

Curiously, Types 2 and 7 often have trouble deciding whether they are a 2 or a 7 because there is so much overlap in the behaviors of the two types. Both are drawn to engaging with others and to having good relations though for different reasons.

While Type 1s may have trouble prioritizing emotions and building strong relationships with others using the techniques of the 2, the 1s can effectively achieve similar results by emulating the dynamics of the fun-seeking 7 and building relationships based on humor, positivity, and enthusiasm. These behaviors are accessible to the 1 along their path of integration.

# Path of Growth for Type 2 Leaders

Type 2s are driven to build strong emotional bonds with others, so imagine how difficult it would be for them to suppress their emotions and feelings like the 3. It would be nearly impossible.

**The Obstacle.** The 2s can be so caught up in their feelings with others that they lose objectivity, which limits their perspective. The hardest behavior for the 2 is suppressing those emotional connections. How can the 2 emulate Type 3's trademark behavior of independent, emotionless objectivity?

**The Way Around: Integrate to Type 4.** As Type 2s move along their path of integration towards Type 4 they lessen their focus on others' feelings, thereby revealing their own. Much like the 4, the integrated 2 can understand and appreciate their own unique reactions and perspectives without being distracted by their connections to others.

Both the 3s and the 4s can be emotionally cool since the suppressed emotion 3s naturally mask their feelings and the internal emotion 4s have learned to mask theirs. Once the integrated 2s have quieted the need to connect with others, they can access the calm, cool, collected demeanor of Types 3 and 4, which enables them to be more objective even in emotional situations.

In problem solving, relieved of the acute focus on others' feelings, the integrated 2 is free to explore their own unique thoughts and feelings and generate novel ideas in much the same way as typical 3s and 4s.

# Path of Growth for Type 3 Leaders

For the suppressed emotion Type 3, the constant roiling feelings of the internal emotion Type 4 are difficult to fathom, making behaviors based on those feelings difficult for the 3 to emulate.

**The Obstacle.** Since the 3s suppress their feelings they are inexperienced at exploring their own emotions, let alone those of others. This situation makes it difficult for them to sense the emotional reactions of others in the way that comes naturally to the 4.

To the 3, an idea is just an idea. Since they do not react emotionally, they can fail to understand how others around them are responding. This is a blind spot for the 3. How can Type 3s learn to acknowledge and appreciate their emotional reactions as well as those of others?

**The Way Around: Integrate to Type 6.** Type 3 can overcome their inability to understand their own internal emotional responses by moving along their path of integration in the direction of Type 6. Type 6s adeptly socialize ideas and assimilate others' emotional reactions to them. Using this same approach, 3s can become attentive to and learn from the emotional cues of others.

Type 6s ask lots of questions. The 3 can use this strategy to engage with others in order to understand their feelings. All the 3 needs to do is ask how someone feels and believe them, even though the 3 may not share the same feelings. Though they do not share the innate emotional sensitivity of Type 4, listening to others describe their feelings can increase a Type 3's awareness of emotional reactions. Conversations help the 3s understand feelings and build empathy. Eventually, understanding others' feelings can help them begin to register their own emotional responses.

# Path of Growth for Type 4 Leaders

Type 4 is the internal emotion type of the Heart-Feeling-Emotion center, while Type 5 is the internal anxiety type of the Head-Thinking-Anxiety center. Moving from Type 4 to Type 5—from heart-centric feeling to head-centric thinking—is challenging for the 4.

**The Obstacle.** The typical 4s are so embroiled in their emotions that they struggle with the linear, logical thinking characteristic of Type 5. Their feelings can be so dominant that it's hard for them to create the quiet mental space required for prolonged, detailed, logical analysis of problems, like Type 5 does.

**The Way Around: Integrate to Type 1.** As Type 4s move along their path of integration, they develop principles of truth and beauty analogous to the dynamic of the 1. The 4s can use those principles as guideposts for analysis and decision making independent of their feelings. Using principles rather than emotional reactions to anchor their reasoning gives Type 4s analytical abilities similar to those of a typical Type 5.

In their secure state, Type 4's analytical abilities can resemble those of Type 1 or Type 5. Also, the calm 4 can become much more aware and observant of their surroundings, like the 5. Along their path of integration, the 4 can emulate many typical Type 5 behaviors.

---

## Career Paths and the Path of Integration

---

At a workshop of Enneagram-aware community leaders, we explored the role dynamics participants use in their professions. We noticed a curious pattern: each of these leaders had assumed roles in their careers that relied on behaviors represented by their respective path of integration types.

For instance, a Type 1 copyeditor had developed the technique of infusing humor in comments to soften the delivery, much like a Type 7 would. A Type 2 had developed a career as a photographer, representing the artistic eye of Type 4. A Type 4 had assumed the role of director of an art department, representing a transition to the dynamics of Type 1. A Type 5 had assumed the role of director of a laboratory, moving into a leadership role typified by Type 8. A Type 6 had moved into the role of program manager, building consensus like the Type 9. Most notably, a Type 8 had become a pastor of a church, providing help for many people, like a typical Type 2.

In each of these cases, the person had moved out of the "comfort zone" of their native type by moving along their path of integration. Following this path had enabled them to readily access and exhibit leadership skills and behaviors necessary for their roles. Fascinatingly, all these leaders were drawn to roles epitomized by the types on their paths of integration!

---

# Path of Growth for Type 5 Leaders

For the internal anxiety Type 5, the hardest behaviors to emulate are those typical of the suppressed anxiety Type 6. These two types are both in the Head-Thinking-Anxiety center, but while Type 5s are masters at collecting and analyzing data they can struggle to match Type 6's decisiveness. Type 5s see the many nuances and shades of gray in the data, and they find it hard to make a decision because of the anxiety-inducing pitfalls lurking in every course of action.

**The Obstacle.** Just as Type 4s are sensitive to the emotional content in their surroundings and roil in their emotional reactions, Type 5s are sensitive to fear and roil with anxiety induced by the possibility of being wrong. Suppressing anxiety allows Type 6s to decide and act. How can 5s quiet their anxiety so they can make a decision?

**The Way Around: Integrate to Type 8.** Type 5's path of integration is towards the decisive Type 8. As the 5s master their data, their anxiety recedes. In their calm, anxiety-minimized state, they can identify satisfactory paths towards a goal and assign probabilities of success (or failure), much like the 6. In this state of mastery, Type 5s can express their analysis and conclusions confidently. Furthermore, they can make decisions based on those conclusions and take action accordingly, much like a typical 6 who has identified the path of least danger.

# Path of Growth for Type 6 Leaders

Simply saying yes to new things can be distressing for Type 6s. Unknown situations cause anxiety, and new things represent many unknowns. As the suppressed anxiety type of the Head-Thinking-Anxiety center, Type 6 needs time to process new situations to assure themselves that risks are manageable. This thoughtful, skeptical behavior can dampen enthusiasm. On the other hand, the 7s' positivity allows them to build enthusiasm and rapport with new people quickly and start having fun right away! For Type 6, the behaviors typical of Type 7 are the hardest to emulate.

**The Obstacle.** The 6s' anxiety blocks them from saying yes and participating fully in new activities. It is difficult for them to act spontaneously and embrace new situations enthusiastically. Until they understand what could happen, Type 6s will be reluctant to participate. Anxiety inhibits their ability to embrace new ideas, directions, activities, and people—behavior that comes easily to the 7s.

**The Way Around: Integrate to Type 9.** As Type 6s move along their path of integration and quiet their anxiety, they are more able to appreciate and anticipate the reactions and desires of those around them. As this happens, the 6s can conform to others more readily, much like a Type 7 would. In their secure state, Type 6's can say yes and go along with the crowd—fully participating in new activities.

In their integrated state Type 6s will also calmly interact with others and become great listeners, seeking to understand opinions and perspectives, which allow them to build rapport with new people. Listening is one of the best tools for building rapport, and asking questions and listening can help the 6 start conversations with strangers, accomplishing what comes easily and naturally to the 7.

---

### Week of "Yes!"

---

As a 6, my natural inclination is to reflexively object to something new, at least until I have thought it through. Unfortunately, this instantaneous negative reaction can be off-putting and chill the mood for others. To combat my instinct, I created a week of "Yes!" every month for each of my kids. I make a concerted effort to start with "Yes!" to whatever idea they propose and do my best to fulfill it. My kids love it, and we all have learned from this.

Recently, I read Shonda Rhimes's book, *Year of Yes*. Rhimes took it one step further and said yes to everything for a year. In her book, she describes how this approach transformed her life. I bet that Shonda Rhimes is a 6! In any case, *Year of Yes* is an instructive book for any 6.

---

# Path of Growth for Type 7 Leaders

The hardest behavior for Type 7 to emulate is the no-nonsense, direct approach of Type 8—especially if that means being confrontational. Type 7 is the external anxiety type of the thinking center, while Type 8 is the external anger type in the intuitive center. Unlike Type 8s, the fun-seeking 7s tend to avoid confrontation at all cost for fear that people will have negative feelings towards them, which would increase their anxiety. The 8s have no such anxious reaction.

**The Obstacle.** The movement from Type 7 to Type 8 transitions from the head-centric thinking center to the gut-centric intuitive center. For the 7, the challenge is to put aside their anxiety and act like the fearless Type 8. Type 7s have trouble confronting others and asserting themselves, even when the situation calls for that behavior. They are so concerned with being liked that they will suppress their own intentions to avoid any negative interaction that might reflect poorly on them. They refrain from assertive Type 8 behaviors in order to avoid negativity.

**The Way Around: Integrate to Type 5.** Anxiety drives the 7s' compulsion to have everyone like them. As Type 7s move along their path of integration towards Type 5, their anxiety recedes—as does the drive to be liked by others. In this state, they can pursue their own interests, independently of others, much like Type 5.

In their secure state, Type 7's demeanor changes from frenetic to calm, allowing them to broaden their perspective. Like the highly rational 5, the 7 can examine the world from all angles—good and bad, positive and negative—and can understand and explain all sides. They acquire the ability to communicate objectively and factually without taking the matter personally. This allows the 7s to exhibit the direct communication style, including the confrontational dynamic, of the fearless Type 8.

# Path of Growth for Type 8 Leaders

For Type 8—the external anger type of the Gut-Intuitive-Anger center—the hardest behaviors to emulate are those typical of the suppressed anger Type 9. Type 8s want to get things done, and if a few feathers are ruffled along the way, so be it. The leap from embracing conflict to avoiding it is daunting for the 8. Because of this, it is difficult for the 8 to emulate the dynamic of the peacemaking 9.

**The Obstacle.** It is hard to imagine Type 8s shying away from a fight as their instinct is to confront any and every challenger. Because of this tendency, the 8s have an exceedingly difficult time adopting Type 9's peacemaking style.

**The Way Around: Integrate to Type 2.** As the 8s feel comfortable and secure in their environment, they move along their path of integration towards the behaviors of Type 2. In the integrated state, they take the time to appreciate the needs of others and work to fulfill those needs. Integrated 8s rise above any immediate conflict and take on a global perspective. They will apply their tremendous energy to benefit others, thus bringing peace to those around them. In this way, they can achieve outcomes like the Type 9.

---

## When You Hold a Hammer, Your World Is a Nail

---

Type 8s are arguably the most confident of all Enneagram types. As a member of the Gut-Intuitive-Anger center, they are not distracted by anxiety like those in the Head-Thinking-Anxiety center or by feelings like those in the Heart-Feeling-Emotion center. Type 8s act assertively, optimistic that they can achieve whatever they pursue.

As an 8, why do you even need to bother accessing the other Enneagram dynamics? If you can get anything you want using your native 8 strategies, why consider other approaches?

As a Type 8 progressing in your career, you may become aware of obstacles that limit your success. Some symptoms of those obstacles are:

- Staff that are overly dependent on you for decision making
- Staff wondering why you are angry at them
- Staff not acting until you tell them what to do

The typical 8 will attribute these symptoms to failures of their staff. The self-aware 8 may realize that they are part of the problem—their own behaviors may be limiting their success. That realization is the 8's first step towards understanding the need for other approaches.

The 8 can be the hammer of the Enneagram. When 8s realize that the hammer is not the best tool for every job, they start to explore other tools, approaches, and dynamics. The 8s who have come to this realization will get the most out of this book. And this book serves as a guide to identify the best tool for the problem-solving task.

---

# Path of Growth for Type 9 Leaders

Type 9s have the hardest time emulating behaviors typical of Type 1. Type 9 is the suppressed anger type of the Gut-Intuitive-Anger center, while Type 1 is the internal anger type. Type 9s are reluctant to assert their own opinion for fear of conflict. Type 1s, on the other hand, are not afraid of asserting their position based on their principles and will defend their position aggressively.

**The Obstacle.** Type 9s want to preserve peace in the environment. They will do almost anything to avoid conflict, including suppressing their own opinions and principles. How can the peace-loving 9 assume Type 1's principled, even confrontational, stance and assert their own opinion?

**The Way Around: Integrate to Type 3.** As 9s move along their path of integration they put their full energy into the community, appearing like an energetic Type 3. Often, they surround themselves with like-minded teammates who share similar goals. In this environment, the 9s can express their own desires and work towards achieving them.

Integrated 9s will absorb the principles of their community, and they will pursue those principles with righteousness and a lower regard for the feelings of others—much like the approach of Type 1. In their secure state, Type 9s learn that it is not their responsibility to appease everyone. They can assert their own opinions without worrying how others may react, thereby achieving behavior similar to that of Type 1.

# The Leadership Behaviors Challenge

As a leader, you want a full set of tools at your disposal. The Enneagram describes nine dynamics you can access, some with ease and some with more effort. As you embark on a journey along your path of integration, the dynamics of the other Enneagram types become easier for you to access.

For each Enneagram type, the next type in the clockwise direction typically represents the most challenging dynamic, especially those behaviors necessary for the corresponding step in problem solving.

Your path of integration provides a workaround that allows high-speed freeway access to your bumpy, two-lane highway behaviors.

## Personal Coach

If you seek guidance on your personal path of growth, I suggest that you consider a coach whose dynamics lie on your path of integration. A coach with those Enneagram dynamics can both instruct and model behaviors that will help you grow personally and as a leader. I have such a coach, and the relationship serves me well.

Who are the best candidates for your personal coach? There are (at least) two strong options. The first is a person whose native type is the type on your path of integration. The second is a person with *your* type who has moved along the path of integration and spends most of their time in the integrated state. This latter option is interesting because they can model desired behaviors that are accessible to you as well as share stories of their journey down the path of integration—stories that could inform and help you on your own journey.

Additionally, I have noticed that the pairs of like types and types connected by the paths of integration/disintegration tend to get along well with one another. This tendency bodes well for coaching relationships composed of these pairs.

# Facing Challenges: Your Hero's Journey

Most great stories feature a protagonist faced with a challenge that must be overcome through a personal transformation. Each Enneagram type represents a distinct hero's journey that shows how we react when stressed with a challenge (path of disintegration) and rise up to overcome that challenge (path of integration).

Of course, there is a catch: as the protagonist in your story, you must put in effort. You need to acquire the skills to operate in your most secure state. As we move through our paths of personal growth and transformation, we acquire many new tools with which to face our challenges and overcome our disintegrated behaviors, following our own hero's journey.

While this chapter focused on the benefits of moving along your path of integration, what about the path of disintegration? Chapter 5, "The Creativity Seesaw," explores how swinging between disintegration and integration can stimulate creative contributions to problem solving and explains how each Enneagram type serves a unique role in the creative process.

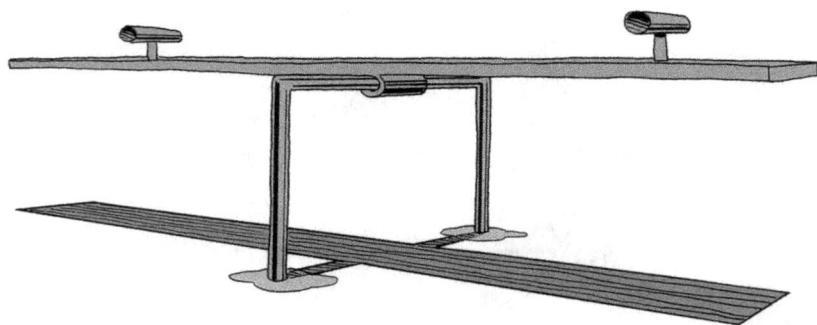

# CHAPTER 5

# The Creativity Seesaw

A team manager once told me that he encouraged conflict among team members since competition between approaches produced the best ideas. I was stunned. Sadly, this wasn't the first time I had encountered this management style. And though this approach is antithetical to everything I have come to understand about developing creative and effective teams, I wondered if there was some grain of truth that allowed this myth to persist.

In developing the problem-solving framework described in Chapter 2, "Problem Solving with the Enneagram," on page 63, I realized that each step requires creative contributions. Each Enneagram dynamic brings unique and valuable creative energy to the process. Additionally, the creative contribution of each Enneagram type is suited for the respective step in the problem-solving process.

What drives these distinct, creative contributions, and how does the Enneagram describe that driving force?

The answer lies in the movement of the Enneagram types along their paths of integration and disintegration. Along one path we are more open to receiving inspiration, and along the other we act on that inspiration. Like a seesaw, each type moves back and forth along the paths, and I believe this motion drives creativity.

Take cooking as an example. Say you are working with a familiar recipe but do not have all the ingredients at hand. Not having time to run to the store, you improvise and substitute other ingredients. You have created a new dish! Is this not a creative act?

The creative impulse strikes most acutely when we are forced to act outside our normal pattern. Type 8 exemplifies this principle well. The 8's normal inclination is to act. Let's say an 8 is cooking a meal for their family. The cook reaches for that important ingredient and realizes it's not in the kitchen. This restrains the 8's default state—acting. In that moment of restraint, the space opens for the Type 8 to intuit an idea to overcome the immediate problem. That moment of restraint can be represented by motion along the 8's path of disintegration and towards behaviors resembling the quiet, contemplative Type 5. Since this ideation can be an unconscious process for the 8, they may not associate their intuition with creativity—although I assert it is. Having overcome the problem, they slip back into action, in this case motivated by the desire to feed their family—behavior that resembles the Helper Type 2 along the 8's path of integration.

Creativity is not merely the generation of an original idea but the entire process, including the actions that manifest the idea into the world. The impulse to act on the new idea is as important as the idea itself; both are critical ingredients.

In the context of the Enneagram, the creative process involves three steps:

1) Motivation
2) Ideation (Inspiration)
3) Action (Perspiration)

Each Enneagram type has a unique motivating driver. As a quick refresher, here is a brief summary of the nine motivations.

**Table 5.1 – Motivations by Enneagram Type**

| Type | Motivation |
|:---:|:---|
| 1 | Right wrongs, get things "right" |
| 2 | Receive appreciation |
| 3 | Be acknowledged for accomplishments and successes |
| 4 | Be recognized for unique perspectives |
| 5 | Collect resources, not be perceived as uninformed |
| 6 | Know what is going to happen |
| 7 | Be adored by everyone |
| 8 | Secure control of their environment |
| 9 | Eliminate discord in their environment |

The underlying motivation for each Enneagram type is the fuel that powers us along our paths of integration and disintegration. When our motivating drives are blocked, we increasingly move towards insecurity along our path of disintegration. When we quiet our motivating compulsion, we can move towards security along our path of integration.

Inspiration looks different for each type. Often, we equate inspiration with an idea, but is there a more general way to treat inspiration? For those in the thinking center, there is a clear connection between inspiration, ideas, and thoughts, which is not necessarily true for those in the other centers. People in the intuitive center can be inspired to action without ever consciously contemplating the idea that informs their action; they simply act on their intuition. In the feeling center, inspiration comes in the form of feelings. In all cases, I think inspiration is better defined as a goal.

By expanding our understanding of inspiration and motivation, we discover that each type contributes to the creative process in its own unique way. Since the Enneagram directly addresses our motivations and our swings between security and insecurity, I propose using the Enneagram to describe a framework for the creative process: the Creativity Seesaw.

**The Creativity Seesaw**

# The Duality of Creativity

The creative process involves an inspiration state and an action state. The Enneagram type determines whether inspiration occurs in the integrated, secure state or in the disintegrated, insecure state, with action occurring in the complementary state. The underlying motivation for creativity lies at the core of each type—the fulcrum of the Creativity Seesaw. The differences in how these forces interact mean that each type contributes uniquely to the creative process.

Insecurity brought on by need can prompt creativity and invention, at least to a point. If we become too stressed—if our amygdala becomes too activated, releasing adrenaline and cortisol and cutting off access to our prefrontal cortex—then our creativity becomes impaired. Daniel Goleman refers to this as *amygdala hijack* in his book *Emotional Intelligence*. High-stress, high-conflict work environments will diminish your team's creativity.

For the creative process to blossom there must also be space for a state of calm. There is a duality to creativity: goal and action, inspiration and perspiration, insecurity and security, stress and calm. Using the seesaw as a metaphor for the creative process, here is an example of how the creative dynamic works:

*Stress See:* Posed with a problem or challenge, a need arises that you must address.

*Calm Saw:* You sleep on the problem and, in your calm state, generate a possible solution which occurs to you when you awake or when you are in the shower the next morning.

*Stress See:* Now you need to implement the proposal by acting on your idea.

*Calm Saw:* You are relieved that you are making progress, moving towards resolving the problem.

*Stress See:* You encounter an obstacle preventing you from reaching your goal and requiring that you take a new direction.

*Calm Saw:* You sleep on the new problem, and so on.

This seesaw effect drives creativity. How does the Enneagram fit in? Each Enneagram type has its own distinct Creativity Seesaw, oscillating on either side of the normal state between stress and calm. That oscillation propels creativity in each type. By understanding this seesaw mechanism, you can identify how each Enneagram type can contribute creatively to your problem-solving efforts.

Let's examine each Enneagram type in turn. For each, I will highlight the behaviors accessed along the paths of integration and disintegration.

# Creativity Seesaw – Type 1

Type 1
Inspiration:
Understanding
what is missing
(Disintegration
to Type 4)

Type 1 Action:
Inspiring others
to right wrongs
(Integration
to Type 7)

Type 1 Motivation:
Needing to right wrongs

The underlying motivation for Type 1 is to right the perceived wrongs. When perceiving a wrong, the 1 enters the insecure state along their path of disintegration, a movement towards the behaviors of Type 4.

Type 4s *feel* what is lacking or missing in the environment and communicate that feeling in an emotionally impactful way. The 1 behaves similarly when they communicate their intuition about right and wrong, using emotionally powerful words like *shouldn't* and *should*: "The world shouldn't be this way; it should be that way." When using the word *should*, they are describing what they perceive as missing.

The Type 4 dynamic is fertile soil for creativity, and Type 1 has direct access to this soil in the stress state. For the 1, this access manifests as an acute, even emotional, awareness that something in the environment is wrong. That acute awareness is the inspiration state of the Type 1 seesaw. Faced with this wrong, Type 1s are inspired to formulate a vision of how the world should be, free of any wrongs. This is their creative spark.

While in their insecure state, Type 1s have difficulty focusing on anything other than the problem itself. They may dwell on the problem, even revel in it. As they fully grasp the problem and visualize how to rectify it, they move towards their secure state and begin to adopt the dynamic of Type 7. A gift of Type 7 is the ability to listen to others, embrace new ideas, and synthesize those ideas into a plan; the 7 generates enthusiasm for the plan to overcome the problem.

Likewise, in their secure state Type 1s can move into action to solve the problem. The creative duality for Type 1 is a tendency towards inaction and inspiration in the insecure state (disintegration to Type 4) and productive action in the secure state (integration to Type 7).

Type 1s find that their creative talents are best applied to roles that require a high degree of precision. For instance, I often find that 1s assume the role of chief financial officer, where accuracy to the penny is required. They are often drawn to roles in medicine, science, and engineering. Organizations recognize the 1s' tireless pursuit of perfection and often encourage them to take on leadership roles.

# Creativity Seesaw – Type 2

Type 2 Inspiration:
Tapping into
feelings, especially
their own
(Integration
to Type 4)

Type 2 Action:
Acting to help
others
(Disintegration
to Type 8)

Type 2 Motivation:
Needing appreciation

While typical 2s have a great sense for the feelings and reactions of those around them, they can have difficulty accessing their own emotional needs. When Type 2s move towards their secure, integrated state, they tap into the dynamic of Type 4. In the secure state, the 2s, like 4s, can readily identify their own feelings and emotional reactions. Also, like the 4s, they can see what is missing. With that inspiration, they can fashion the missing element in an emotionally impactful way like the typical 4 but often in a way that elicits maximal appreciation from a target audience.

With the missing element identified but with the new opportunity for appreciation as yet unfulfilled, the 2 moves towards insecurity and the dynamic of Type 8 along their path of disintegration. Type 8 is the type most associated with action. In this dynamic, the 2 will work diligently, even aggressively, until they realize their aim and receive the needed appreciation from their target audience.

Type 2s will swing from disintegration back to integration when they either receive appreciation or give up pursuing unfulfilled appreciation from their target and go back to serving their own needs. In either case, they can again move along their path of integration for another spark of inspiration.

For Type 2, the insecure state is characterized by the action-oriented Type 8, and the secure state is characterized by the emotionally connected reactive Type 4. This differs from the Type 1 seesaw; inspiration emerges from the calm state, and action arises from the stress state.

The particular motivation of 2s draws them to roles where they can use their creative talents to help others. They find unique ways to contribute. Their desire to interact with others often lands them in customer-oriented roles; they enjoy sales roles and service roles such as teaching, nursing, and the military. The connection to Type 4 on their path of integration can draw them to artistic endeavors.

# Creativity Seesaw – Type 3

Type 3 Inspiration:
Seeking how
best to appease
(Disintegration
to Type 9)

Type 3 Action:
Systematically
achieving goals
(Integration
to Type 6)

Type 3 Motivation:
Receiving acknowledgment for success

Type 3s seek acknowledgment for their accomplishments. If they are not being recognized or if they are on a project which they sense will fail, the 3 tends to move along their path of disintegration towards the dynamic of Type 9.

In insecurity (when they are actively seeking recognition), the 3 becomes hypersensitive to the opinions of others, resembling the behaviors of Type 9. Because the 3s suppress emotion and can remain cool under pressure, they can readily generate novel ideas even in this stressed state; they will throw out ideas and attentively watch those around them to see how they respond, to see which ideas stick. The 3s will lean towards the ideas that others find favorable, expecting that they will receive the highest accolades for implementing those ideas.

With a path towards success identified, the 3s calm down and move along their path of integration where they exhibit the systematic drive of Type 6, wanting to put people and processes in place. The

6 does this to increase predictability, while the 3 does it to get things done quickly and efficiently—similar behaviors with different underlying motivation. The 3s work tirelessly until their mission is accomplished and they are recognized for their success.

Type 3s receive inspiration from their insecure state, a reactive state characterized by Type 9. They move to action in their secure state, characterized by Type 6.

In their profession, the 3s' pursuit of success draws them to executive and management roles regardless of the field. Their ability to position themselves for success enables them to excel in marketing roles. Their eye for what looks good lends itself to roles in design. They like roles where their creativity can be easily measured—the number of wins for a litigator, the number of tax returns filed for an accountant, or the size of the portfolio for a money manager.

---

## Johnny on the Spot

---

During a team-building activity at work, four of us were on an assembly line to build hamburgers made of plastic parts: bun, burger, lettuce, cheese, and tomato. The goal was to correctly build as many burgers as possible in a given period of time; a machine counted the number of correctly made burgers. We began by making each person responsible for a certain ingredient—the bun person, the burger person, etc. As the activity began, we all started working earnestly on our given task.

One person noticed that our success rate of completed burgers was not high, and on the fly he instructed everyone to switch tactics. He had everyone build a complete burger in their hands before placing it on the conveyor belt. Although not every spot on the belt was taken, every burger on the belt was 100 percent complete. Our success rate shot up, and our team ended up winning the competition.

The person who spoke up was a Type 3. This activity gave me insight into the 3's ability to improvise while under stress. While everyone else was focused on the activity, the 3 was focused on success and thereby motivated to make any changes necessary to achieve the win.

---

# Creativity Seesaw – Type 4

Type 4 Inspiration:
Intense feelings
for what is missing
(Disintegration
to Type 2)

Type 4 Action:
Expressing the void,
what is "wrong"
(Integration
to Type 1)

Type 4 Motivation:
Receiving recognition for unique perspectives

Type 4s carry within them a hidden world of feelings and emotions. Their most intense emotions are evoked by what they perceive as missing or lacking. They demonstrate their unique perspectives when they point out what others can't see. Being recognized for unique perspectives is a motivating force for the 4s.

The 4s' need to pine for what is missing can drive them towards disintegration, resulting in intense emotional feelings. Down this path, the 4s' behaviors can appear like those of the outwardly emotional

Type 2. In the insecure state, Type 4s develop ever more acute feelings of what is missing; feeling the void is the creative spark for the 4.

Once inspired, Type 4s move towards action in their secure, integrated state, represented by the dynamic of Type 1. Type 1s are compelled to action in order to right perceived wrongs. In their secure state, the 4s act by communicating their perceived voids, often in artistic ways. Thereby, their inspiration becomes a creative product. They show the world what is missing and how the world could be.

Type 4s can feel blocked from creativity when they are not being challenged or stimulated. They feel most creative when they are reacting to something in the environment. Moments of reaction can prompt their strongest creative instincts.

Type 4s are drawn to roles where they can express themselves and make an emotional impact. Typical pursuits include art, music, and poetry. They may also take roles in marketing, where they can formulate emotionally impactful messages about an organization, its products, or its services. They often serve in sales roles since they are highly empathetic and can communicate on an emotional level with customers.

## Moving from Right to Left

Moving from Type 4 to Type 5, we leave the right side of the Enneagram and move to the left side. Note that the entire Heart-Feeling-Emotion center (the 2-3-4 triad) is on the right side while the entire Head-Thinking-Anxiety center (5-6-7) is on the left. In other words, the right side of the diagram tends to be driven by emotions while the left tends to be driven by logic. Curiously, this overlaps with the popular concept of "right-brained" and "left-brained." (We will examine the connection between the Enneagram and the brain in Chapter 7, "Work Team Triads: Two Balanced Brains," on page 201.)

Coming from the perspective of Type 6, I find that right-side Enneagram types tend to be much more flexible in their thinking, able to bounce from idea to idea and concept to concept in a nonlinear fashion. On the other hand, left-side Enneagram types tend to construct thoughts in a more linear fashion. Let's examine how these traits play out in the creative process.

## Creativity Seesaw – Type 5

Type 5 Inspiration: Incessantly searching for ideas and mastering information (Type 7 Disintegration)

Type 5 Action: Asserting themselves and acting with confidence (Type 8 Integration)

Type 5 Motivation: Collecting resources and appearing well informed

While we relate Type 4s' creativity to their expression of art, music, poetry, and paintings, we associate the creativity of Type 5s with scientific discovery and innovation. Type 5s can sequester themselves and think deeply about a problem, collecting information, synthesizing ideas, and reliving the problem over and over until they are inspired with a solution.

Along their path of disintegration, Type 5s *abhor* the thought of being considered uninformed. Whereas Type 3s are driven by the positive desire to be recognized for success, Type 5s are motivated by their anxiety about being considered ignorant. This anxiety tends to drive the 5s to focus narrowly and very, very deeply on a target subject matter. As they master their subject, they are able to synthesize information and generate novel ideas, behaviors typical of Type 7.

As the 5s become confident in their subject matter mastery, their anxiety recedes. They relax into the secure state and move on their path of integration towards behaviors of Type 8. In this state, they will challenge the ideas of others and assert their own ideas. In that process, so common in the dialogue of the scientific community, the 5 can share novel ideas and develop them among their peers. Also, the Type 8 dynamic represents action and acting on ideas. In their secure state, Type 5s also have access to this dynamic.

For the 5s, inspiration occurs in the insecure state while they collect and synthesize information, behaviors typical to Type 7. Action occurs in the secure state, when Type 5s assert and act on their ideas, behaviors typical of Type 8.

In their professions, I see 5s exercise their creative strengths in endeavors that require deep knowledge and study. They are drawn to roles in academia, science, engineering, and finance, among others.

# Creativity Seesaw – Type 6

| Type 6 Inspiration: Envisioning systems that work for everyone (Type 9 Integration) | | Type 6 Action: Working diligently to address their sources of anxiety (Type 3 Disintegration) |
|---|---|---|

Type 6 Motivation:
Knowing what is going to happen in order to reduce their anxiety

Type 6s seek predictability; they want to know what is going to happen. When circumstances become uncertain, their anxiety increases and they move along their path of disintegration, exhibiting a tireless drive to address the source of the anxiety. This tireless drive resembles behavior of a typical Type 3, though the 6 is motivated by anxiety while the 3 is motivated by success. In the stressed state, the 6's focus narrows, and they work hard to restore order and predictability to their environment.

As 6s begin to understand the cause-and-effect relationships and address the causes of anxiety, the wave of anxiety begins to recede, revealing new thoughts and ideas. The secure 6 moves along their path of integration towards Type 9, where they are able to appreciate how their ideas will affect the community. The 6 shares promising ideas, gets feedback, and makes determinations about which ideas are most likely to succeed.

Once promising ideas are identified, the 6 feels a sense of urgency to implement those ideas and finally know whether the ideas will work. With the increasing sense of urgency, their anxiety levels rise, and once again they travel along the path of disintegration, working furiously to implement the ideas and relieve their anxiety.

The 6 seesaws from idea generation and socialization on their path of integration to idea implementation and action on their path of disintegration.

In their profession, I see 6s exercise their unique creative muscle in roles in which they can implement processes and systems that deliver predictable outcomes, such as financial controller, program manager, systems engineer, and quality engineer, among others.

## Creativity Seesaw – Type 7

Type 7 Inspiration: Synthesizing information, generating novel ideas (Integration to Type 5)

Type 7 Action: Working dogmatically to promote ideas (Disintegration to Type 1)

Type 7 Motivation: Being adored by everyone

Type 7s are motivated to be liked, even adored, by those around them. Being liked reduces their anxiety. As long as everyone is happy with them, their anxiety goes down. The compulsion of the 7 to interact with others enables them to serve as pollinators of ideas, picking up ideas from their conversations, synthesizing those ideas, and then sharing them with others. To others, the 7s are a veritable font of positive, new ideas. The 7's natural optimism and enthusiasm are contagious; as such, people are receptive to the ideas they promote.

In their secure state, the 7 moves along their path of integration towards the behaviors of Type 5. Like a typical 5, the secure 7 can quietly and calmly contemplate information and ideas that they have collected. Type 7s excel at synthesizing information and developing new ideas—ideas that are often intended to enthuse others. With new ideas at the ready, the 7 moves back into the environment to promote those ideas. For the 7, the secure state towards Type 5 is the state of inspiration.

Curiously, when others embrace the ideas, the 7 may feel as though expectations have been set to deliver on those ideas, and their anxiety levels rise as they are confronted with the need to meet those expectations. Rising anxiety levels cause Type 7s to move along their path of disintegration towards Type 1. In their insecure state, they can become sensitive and single-minded, behaviors resembling those of Type 1. The anxiety in their insecure state can also lead to a frenetic energy which drives the 7s all the more to action—to get out and understand how best to fulfill expectations.

As expectations are met and people become happy both with the outcomes and with the 7s themselves, the anxiety recedes. They move back to security where they can absorb, synthesize, and promote more new ideas.

Type 7s excel at roles that involve promotion where they can use their creative talents for finding ideas that excite others. Type 7s are often drawn to roles in marketing, product management, politics, and the clergy. Organizations embrace their enthusiastic energy and often promote 7s to leadership roles in which their promotional talents serve them well.

# Creativity Seesaw – Type 8

Type 8 Inspiration:
Being restrained
from action
and scanning
opportunities
(Disintegration
to Type 5)

Type 8 Action:
Acting to help
themselves
and others
(Integration
to Type 2)

Type 8 Motivation:
Securing control of their environment

There is a stark difference between Type 8s and Type 7s in their respective tendencies towards action (Type 8) or discussion (Type 7). One of Type 8's defining characteristics is the compulsion to act, whereas a defining characteristic of the 7s is the compulsion to speak. The Type 8 dynamic is the embodiment of acting on ideas.

Curiously, Type 8s often describe "creativity" as generating ideas. They often don't equate their intuition with creativity, thereby downplaying their own contributions. Also, action comes so naturally to the 8s that they may fail to appreciate how important action is to the creative process. Yet, without Type 8's drive to act, many innovative ideas would never come to fruition.

Type 8s' inspiration happens most acutely in moments of restraint. The 8s' restraint occurs along their path of disintegration, resembling behaviors of Type 5. Type 8s are motivated to secure and control their environment. When they feel that they have lost control, their instinct is to step back and seek opportunities to regain it. In these moments of restraint, the window opens for novel ideas to enter.

Because they are in the intuitive center, the 8s' ideas can emerge without their conscious awareness. (This may be another reason why they tend to downplay their own creative instincts.) Once they intuit how to regain control, they move into action. As the 8s make progress, they begin to move along their path of integration towards the dynamic of Type 2. In the integrated state, the 8 uses their tremendous energy to help and support others, creating a secure environment for all.

In their integrated state, the 8s will shine in their instincts to act. They will work tirelessly to implement the plan, at least until they encounter an obstacle. At that point, the 8 moves back to the insecure, non-active space until the next idea emerges, seesawing back and forth in their creative dynamic.

Type 8s excel in roles that require decisiveness, action, and confrontation. They tend to be self-confident, and people naturally follow their lead. Type 8s exert their creative energy by acting on ideas and bringing them to fulfillment, often fighting for the good of their team or community. In organizations, they often take roles in production and operations. Organizations appreciate their drive and decisiveness and promote them to management positions. In law, they often become litigators where they can creatively fight for their clients.

# Tsunamiball

I know a Type 8 individual who was moved by the tsunami in Fukushima, Japan, in March 2011. Watching events in the media from the US, he was shocked by the complete loss of control of the environment.

Reacting to those scenes, he was inspired to create a means by which a family could withstand and survive the ravages of a tsunami. He conceived of a capsule that a family could enter in case of a tsunami and ride out the wave securely within the vessel.

With the idea at hand, the 8 moved into action and started building the vessel, which he calls the "Tsunamiball." The effort an 8 will put into a project that will allow them to secure control of their environment is awe-inspiring. The thought and effort that the 8 put into this vessel clearly illustrates the extent to which an 8 will go. The vessel now stands in his backyard. You can review the entire project at www.tsunamiball.com.

This story illustrates the Creativity Seesaw of the 8, reacting to the loss of control of the environment along the path of disintegration (Type 5) and regaining control and finding a way to help others along the path of integration (Type 2).

# Creativity Seesaw – Type 9

Type 9 Inspiration: Understanding the cause and nature of discord (Disintegration to Type 6)

Type 9 Action: Actively creating a harmonious environment (Integration to Type 3)

Type 9 Motivation: Eliminating discord

When feeling insecure, Type 9s move along their path of disintegration towards Type 6. Much as the 6 becomes hypersensitive in chaotic situations, the 9 becomes hypersensitive when there is discord in their environment. In this state, the 9 will diminish their own perspectives and opinions, resembling the behavior of the 6 when they defer to authority. The gift of the 9 is to listen attentively and to understand the cause of the disagreement. In that state, they are inspired to generate ideas that mitigate the discord and to share those ideas with the aggrieved parties.

As the tension dissolves, the Type 9 relaxes and moves towards the dynamic of Type 3, in which they implement solutions that prevent future discord. They will think through various measures that enhance harmony for all and will work with others to put those measures into place.

When working with their community to implement solutions, discord inevitably arises. The stress causes the 9 to move again along their path of disintegration, where they listen attentively to understand the source of disagreements and generate ideas to ameliorate the situation. As they grow calm, they move back along their path of integration towards Type 3 and work energetically to put the new ideas to work for the good of all. This illustrates the Creativity Seesaw for Type 9.

Ironically, Type 9s can be most creative when put into conflict-rich environments, which continually stimulate them to invent ideas to harmonize the situation. Type 9s are often drawn to service-oriented roles such at customer service and IT in which they excel at calming their customers and resolving their problems. They are great at anticipating stumbling blocks for teams and will often serve in management and project management roles. The leadership style of Type 9 is a perfect fit for consensus-driven organizations.

## The Creativity Seesaw

In each of us there is an engine of creativity that manifests itself differently depending on our Enneagram type. Table 5.2 summarizes these inclinations towards inspiration and action along each type's paths of integration and disintegration.

Based on my understanding of the Enneagram and the dynamics of each type, I find that some types "are inspired" in disintegration and "act" in integration. For others, it is the opposite. Frankly, I find it comforting to know that there is variation in this pattern. When we work together collectively, this diversity of responses allows us to more effectively address any challenge.

## Table 5.2 – Inspiration and Action by Type

| Type | Inspiration | Action |
|:---:|:---:|:---:|
| 1 | Insecurity (Type 4) | Security (Type 7) |
| 2 | Security (Type 4) | Insecurity (Type 8) |
| 3 | Insecurity (Type 9) | Security (Type 6) |
| 4 | Insecurity (Type 2) | Security (Type 1) |
| 5 | Insecurity (Type 7) | Security (Type 8) |
| 6 | Security (Type 9) | Insecurity (Type 3) |
| 7 | Security (Type 5) | Insecurity (Type 1) |
| 8 | Insecurity (Type 5) | Security (Type 2) |
| 9 | Insecurity (Type 6) | Security (Type 3) |

Each step in problem solving requires creative contributions, and each Enneagram type brings a unique, valuable, creative energy to that work. These unique contributions highlight one more facet of the importance of having teams with diverse Enneagram types.

The Creativity Seesaw acknowledges the contribution that stress can play in the creative process. It also illustrates the importance of the calm state. Too much stress can lead to emotional hijacking in which your seesaw gets stuck and the creative process breaks down. Leaders who challenge their teams while creating low-stress work environments can create the playgrounds in which everyone's creativity seesaws can swing freely.

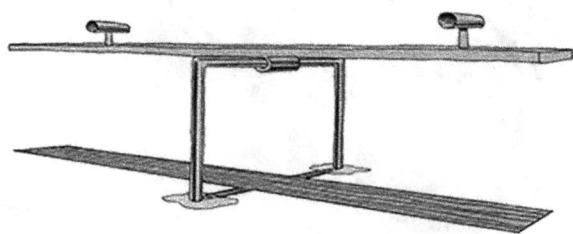

# CHAPTER 6

# The Enneagram and Time

Mañana, mañana—that is what I thought when I woke up this morning. After all, it is Saturday, and I have made great progress writing this week. Then I thought, "Well, I did promise myself to write this weekend. And I am waking up at my usual time to write. And I have only given myself a month to write this book." With that, I was up, out of bed, and—with coffee at hand—writing this chapter.

Each Enneagram type has a different sense of time. These differences color how we view the world, how we interact with people, and how we go about our daily activities. They allow us to complement one another's perspectives, and sometimes they can lead to conflict.

Over the years as I have explored the Enneagram with friends, family, and clients, I have observed patterns and tendencies in how each Enneagram type relates to time. In this chapter, I will share these insights and propose a model showing how each type processes time. I will also explore how each type's perspective contributes to our collective human ability to solve problems and how that dynamic is well suited to the corresponding step in problem solving.

Finally, I will share some strategies project managers can use to instill a sense of urgency about upcoming deadlines specific to each Enneagram type. These strategies will help you keep your project on track.

Once you understand how each team member processes time, you will understand how everyone can work together to solve problems quickly and efficiently. Time can serve as the wizard behind the curtain, a motivating force to propel your project forward.

## Past, Present, or Future?

Two aspects of time come into play when thinking about how each Enneagram type relates to time. One can be described by a timeline that shows the points in time where each type devotes a large portion of mental energy: past, present, or future.

Some of us focus our energy on the very next thing in front of us—the *immediate future*. Some of us dwell on possibilities of what could happen further out in time. I call that either *near future* or *distant future*, depending on how far into the future it is.

On the other hand, some of us spend time at different points in the past—*immediate past, near past,* and *distant past*—and some of us live right in the *present*. Below I describe my observations of where each Enneagram type falls on the timeline and why I think that happens. I call this the Mental Energy Timeline (Figure 6.1).

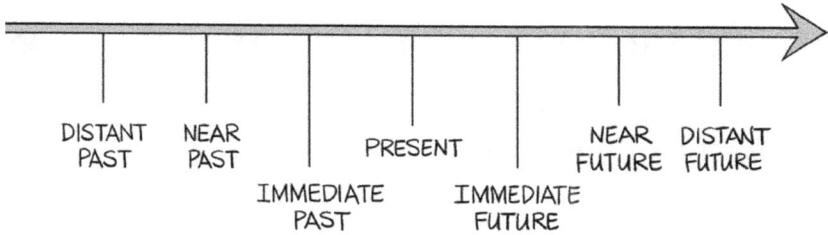

**Figure 6.1 – Mental Energy Timeline**

# Time as a Commodity

The other aspect of time that comes into play is how much or little time we think we have (i.e., thinking of time as a commodity). Think back to my opening anecdote about getting out of bed on a Saturday morning. I might have stayed in bed if I perceived that there was still plenty of time to get to my writing and there was no rush. However, I rarely think like that. Rather, I felt like there was not enough time to meet a project goal and that getting out of bed (at 5 a.m.) would get me a couple of hours that I would not have had otherwise.

This scenario illustrates how at times we can feel that there is not enough time, and sometimes we feel that there is plenty of time. In my observations, feelings about time vary by Enneagram type. Some Enneagram types perceive an abundance of time while others perceive scarcity, and those perceptions color each type's sense of urgency. For those who perceive scarcity, time becomes a motivating force to act with urgency. Those who perceive abundance have more patience; time itself is not a motivating force.

In the following sections I will share my observations of where each Enneagram type lands on the Mental Energy Timeline and whether each has a stronger sense of urgency or patience. First, let's examine the Mental Energy Timeline.

# Mental Energy Timeline by Enneagram Type

Each Enneagram type will reference time in a distinct way. We will examine both *where* along the timeline each type focuses and *why* they focus there.

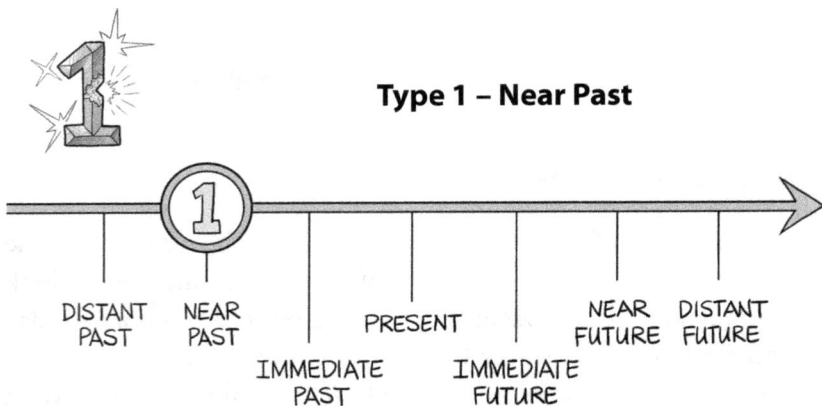

**Type 1 – Near Past**

DISTANT PAST    NEAR PAST    IMMEDIATE PAST    PRESENT    IMMEDIATE FUTURE    NEAR FUTURE    DISTANT FUTURE

Type 1s look at what is right in front of them and compare that to a model they have constructed of what is "right" and "wrong." The 1s can expend a great deal of energy collecting information to complete their model of what constitutes perfectly solving a given problem. They will not be satisfied until they have assured themselves that they have collected all available information regarding the problem.

Then, while they are analyzing the problem at hand, they continually refer to the model they have constructed. Remember, Type 1s do not want to be wrong and will go to great lengths to arm themselves with any and all information to avoid being proven wrong. If they are ever shown to be wrong, the first excuse Type 1s will give is that they did not have all the information or that somehow the information changed after they examined it.

Type 1s tend to be the most ideological of all Enneagram types—having ideologies and belief systems that are built up over time. Their ideological frameworks serve as reference points against which they can compare and judge current situations.

How does this relate to the Mental Energy Timeline? The behavior of Type 1s as they refer back to their models of right and wrong illustrates how they are spending time in the past. Since they are not necessarily thinking about the immediate past or the distant past, I refer to this point on the timeline as the near past—the point from which the 1 compares the current situation to models they have developed.

## Type 2 – Distant Past

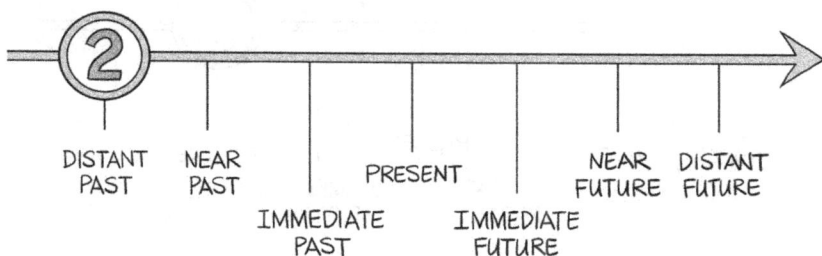

Type 2s love to tell stories. The story often starts, "I remember when Mary, John, and I were working on a big account, and ..." They are recalling the emotional bonds that they developed over the course of some past experience. They use those emotional experiences—good and bad—to guide them on their current journey.

Reminiscing is a way for Type 2s to keep emotions front and center. They use this strategy to build and strengthen emotional bonds with others, even when they are interacting with them in the present. This behavior puts Type 2s in the distant past along the Mental Energy Timeline—even further in the past than Type 1s.

Type 2's strong memories of the past can serve teams in at least two ways. First, they will likely know people from their past who could help the team with its current challenge, and they will often be eager to reconnect and rekindle those emotional bonds.

Second, having vivid memories of the past allows them to relate a current situation to past experiences and advise the team on what will and won't work. They can inform the team to avoid pitfalls and achieve desirable outcomes.

## Type 3 – Near Future

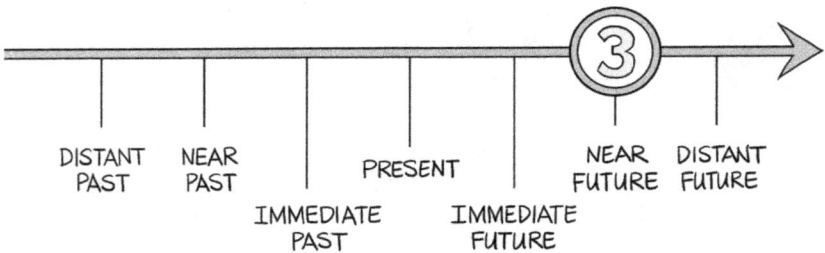

DISTANT PAST   NEAR PAST   IMMEDIATE PAST   PRESENT   IMMEDIATE FUTURE   NEAR FUTURE   DISTANT FUTURE

While Type 1s and Type 2s are referencing the past, Type 3s move us into the future by envisioning success. They see challenges as opportunities to demonstrate their capabilities. This demonstration can take many forms. Certainly, it can be the successful outcome of a project, but it can also be excellence at tomorrow's presentation.

This desire to portray their achievements leads Type 3s to think about how people will react to them in the future. They expend a great deal of mental energy on future outcomes. They are not necessarily thinking about the next thing on their plate. They are thinking several steps ahead—to a successful outcome and how they will get there quickly and efficiently.

Since the focus of the 3 lies somewhere between the immediate future and the distant future, I call this point on the Mental Energy Timeline the near future. This focus helps keep teams looking forward and on the right track towards success.

## Type 4 – Present "Reacting"

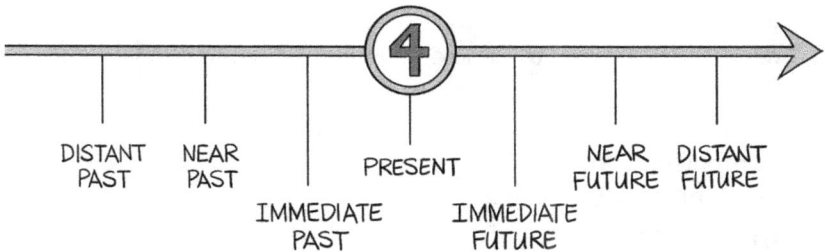

| DISTANT PAST | NEAR PAST | | PRESENT | | NEAR FUTURE | DISTANT FUTURE |
|---|---|---|---|---|---|---|
| | | IMMEDIATE PAST | | IMMEDIATE FUTURE | | |

Type 4 is the first type in our examination that tends to focus on the present. The 4 is constantly reacting to their environment, feeling everything. Type 4s live in the here and now, reacting emotionally to their surroundings.

Since Type 4s tend to react to what is happening in front of them, their focus on the Mental Energy Timeline is in the present. If I were to split hairs, I would put the focus on the instantaneous past since they are reacting to what just happened. But, for simplicity's sake, I just call it present.

Since 4s are so in touch with their own feelings and reactions, they have insights into how others may react as well. This enables them to prepare their teammates for how others will respond emotionally to ideas and stimulus, which is the gift of Type 4s and their contribution to their team.

---

## Where Is Your Focus?

---

Are you thinking about where you focus your own thoughts on the Mental Energy Timeline?

I imagine that you have experienced shifting your focus along this timeline. Who hasn't heard an idea and immediately felt that it was great or terrible? That immediate emotional reaction in the present is what Type 4s feel all the time.

Or, who hasn't envisioned a successful future outcome or a warm memory of a friend from the past? While we all do this at times, or force the feeling if we try, the respective Enneagram type is doing it naturally most of the time, almost as if by design.

---

## Type 5 – Immediate Past

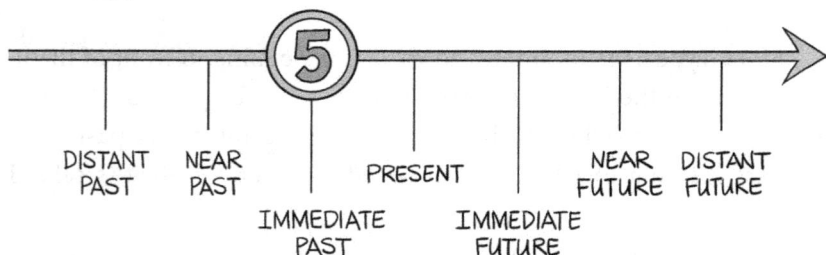

DISTANT PAST    NEAR PAST    IMMEDIATE PAST    PRESENT    IMMEDIATE FUTURE    NEAR FUTURE    DISTANT FUTURE

Type 5s are vigilant observers. If the situation requires, they can focus their powers of observation on what is happening in the present. But, when they do, they are not reacting the way Type 4s do.

Instead, as soon as the situation allows, the 5s retreat with their newly obtained cache of information and begin analyzing, rehashing, and reliving it. For the 5s, the act of reliving what happened can almost feel more real than when they were experiencing it in the moment.

As Type 5s process their information, they extract the interesting and useful nuggets, which they store away for later use. This allows them to secure the information they need to lower their anxiety.

The tendency to mull over recent events puts Type 5s' focus on the Mental Energy Timeline on the immediate past—typically, on information absorbed within the last 24 to 48 hours, and longer if more analysis is required.

Type 5s' ability to dwell on information, analyze it, and dissect it in excruciating detail is the talent they contribute to their team. The 5s can pull out the valuable nuggets at the right time to keep the team from going in the wrong direction. They will speak quietly, so pay close attention when they do!

## Type 6 – Distant Future

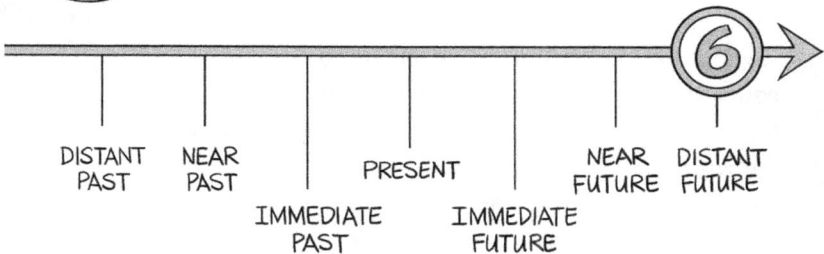

Type 6s want to know what is going to happen, and they do not like to be surprised. As long as they have a sense for the likely outcomes, their anxiety is reduced.

In order for the 6s to anticipate outcomes and associate probabilities with each, they have to play out various scenarios in their mind. Essentially, they are continuously simulating the future. Because of this tendency, I find that Type 6s think the furthest into the future of all Enneagram types. As such, I put the focus of the 6s at distant future on the Mental Energy Timeline, as they work through all possible outcomes.

The focus on the future can be a double-edged sword for the 6. The ability to see into the future and assign probabilities to outcomes is the remarkable talent that helps the 6s and their teams to find the best path forward—the path of least danger that leads to the beautiful world envisioned in Step 1. On the other hand, the 6s' propensity to dwell on the future makes it difficult for them to "live in the moment," which can frustrate those around them.

## Memory Like an Elephant?

Do you have a memory like an elephant? I don't.

My inability to remember the past used to frustrate me. Now, knowing that I am a 6, I am much less frustrated because I understand why my memory is poor.

Type 2s reminisce about the past, reinforcing the neural pathways of their memories; I rarely reminisce. Even when I am having conversations with friends in the present, the most interesting topics for me are about the future! I may be exercising neural pathways for my imagination, but I am not exercising the pathways to my memories.

That tendency makes it difficult for me to remember events in the past. I have to rely on people with much better memories, like my friends who are 2s.

While Type 2s may have a terrific memory, I think Type 6s may struggle to remember.

---

## Type 7 – Immediate Future

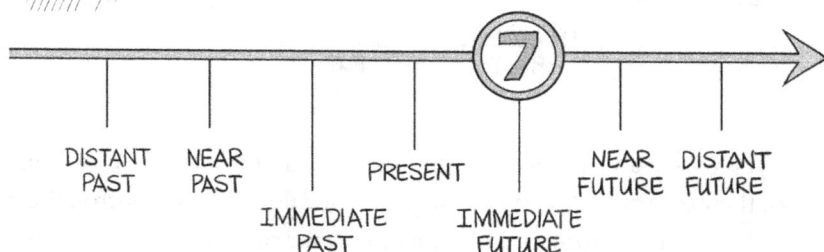

Type 7s want to have fun. When they are not engaged in a fun activity, their minds wander to the next fun thing to do. Because of the 7s' future orientation towards the immediate next activity, I characterize their focus on the Mental Energy Timeline as immediate future.

Type 7s want to make sure that everyone in their environment is happy, especially with them. The strategy for the 7 to keep everyone happy is to engage them in fun activities. They come up with ideas and create visions for how everyone can have fun together, and then they promote those ideas to the group.

The 7 has a talent for creating enthusiasm for ideas and getting everyone on board. This natural ability is their contribution to your team—spurring everyone to action and moving them towards the next destination in the immediate future.

## Type 8 – Present "Acting"

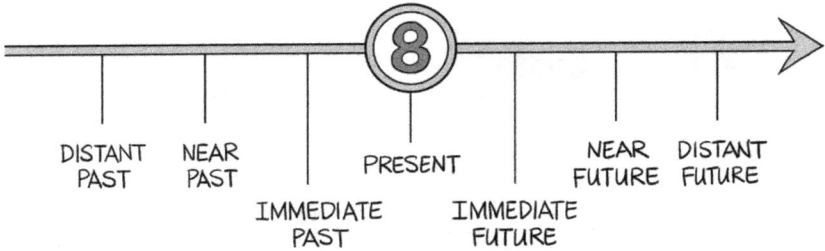

| DISTANT PAST | NEAR PAST | | PRESENT | | NEAR FUTURE | DISTANT FUTURE |
| | | IMMEDIATE PAST | | IMMEDIATE FUTURE | | |

Type 8s are an interesting case. They are motivated to secure control of their environment. When they feel they do not have control, their focus shifts to the future to find a way to regain control. Once they have that plan, the focus shifts to the present in which they act on their plan.

A Type 8 CEO tells me that one of his favorite sayings is, "Staying in the now, looking towards the future." I think this saying sums up nicely the focus of the 8. The 8 wants to have a plan but does not want to overthink it. They want to get started as quickly as possible. If the plan doesn't work out, the focus moves to a new plan, and then quickly back to action. They tend to want to spend most of their time acting in the moment, which is why I put the 8s' focus on the Mental Energy Timeline as present.

Remember that Type 4s are reacting to events that just happened; as such, the focus of the 4 could be described as the *instantaneous past*. In that same vein, Type 8 could be characterized as the *instantaneous future*. They are not reacting to what is happening in the present; instead, they are acting in the present—creating the future, moment by moment, second by second, that will realize their plan. But, for simplicity's sake, I just call it present.

Type 8 pulls teams right into action in the present, and that is their primary contribution to your team. The 8 dynamic wants to GET IT DONE—NOW!

## Type 9 – Immediate Future

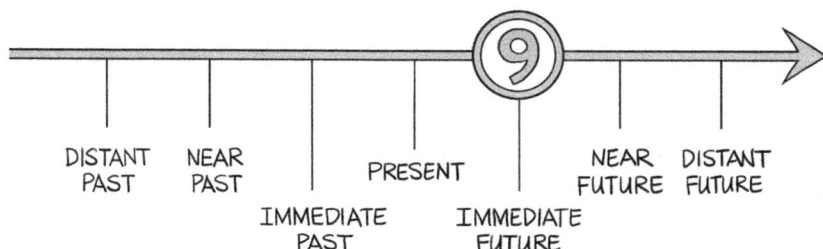

Type 9s sit atop the Enneagram diagram, neither on the right side nor the left. That position gives them a balanced perspective on both the emotional and logical motivations of themselves and others. How does that balanced perspective influence their perception of time?

Type 9s are motivated to minimize conflict and anger in their environment. They do this by continuously anticipating the needs and desires of others and ensuring, as best as possible, that those needs and desires are met. In this manner, they minimize conflict and maintain a harmonious environment. In a way, the motivation of the 9 is the flip side of the 7. While Type 7 endeavors to maximize happiness, Type 9 strives to minimize conflict. Although the motivations are different, the outcomes are often similar.

I placed the 7 at the immediate future along the Mental Energy Timeline, and I put the 9 at that same point. Both are immersed in their environment, anticipating the needs and desires of others and creating an immediate future that is happy (Type 7) and conflict-free (Type 9), respectively.

When Type 9 wakes up in the morning, they are already anticipating the needs and desires of others and formulating plans to maintain peace throughout the day. On a team, these powerful insights help keep everyone on track and moving in the same direction. It is better to be looking towards the goal—the collectively envisioned beautiful world—than glaring at each other in conflict. The 9s' forward-looking anticipation of the immediate future minimizes team conflict and keeps the team on track towards that beautiful world.

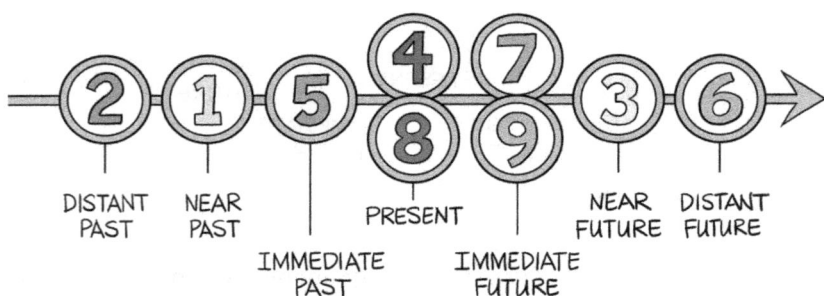

**Figure 6.2 – The Mental Energy Timeline with Types**

# A Timeline Perspective on Problem Solving

The Mental Energy Timeline shows where each Enneagram type tends to focus their mental energy. Each type has a perspective on time that helps the team identify and overcome challenges (Figure 6.2). Here is how I see each type contributing their timeline perspective in problem solving:

- The 1s' ability to reference their model of the near past heightens their awareness of right and wrong and alerts the team to problems in the environment.
- The 2s' ability to tap into distant past feelings informs the team what has worked in the past and who in the community is likely to be emotionally bound to the problem.

- The 3s' ability to envision a successful outcome in the near future enables the team to develop ideas for solutions.
- The 4s' ability to react to ideas in the present informs the team immediately whether or not an idea will deliver the emotional energy necessary to take it to completion.
- The 5s' ability to reflect on information in the immediate past helps the team to work through the pros and cons of each idea.
- The 6s' ability to project each idea into the distant future enables the team to predict which ideas are most likely to succeed.
- The 7s' ability to bring the desirable outcome back to the immediate future creates enthusiasm within the community to proceed.
- The 8s' ability to create urgency to act in the present provides the impetus to execute the plan.
- The 9s' focus on anticipating possible conflicts in the immediate future and working to mitigate those conflicts helps to harmonize the solution with all those affected.

Applying these insights to problem solving, we see that the time perspective changes from step to step, cycling from past to present to future as the team moves through the problem-solving process. Each step in problem solving draws on a different perspective along the timeline. During problem solving, the trend is towards realizing the beautiful world, but it is not a straight line to get there. In addition to envisioning the future, at times the team needs to reflect on the past and at times the team needs to act in the present.

Figure 6.3 illustrates how the team cycles through time perspectives on the Mental Energy Timeline as they move through the problem-solving process.

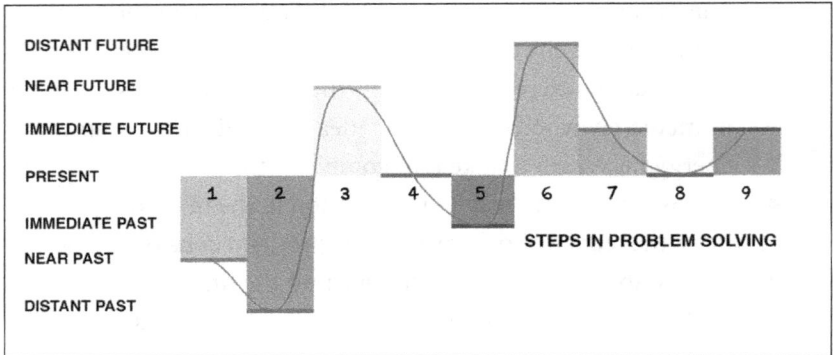

**Figure 6.3 – Time Perspectives during Problem Solving**

I am fascinated by how the focus along the timeline shifts from step to step. While the trend is towards the future, the focus also shifts to the past. The sequence into action is particularly interesting. Step 6 has the team envisioning the path to the end goal in the distant future, Step 7 promotes the plan to get everyone enthused to take the first step forward into the immediate future, and Step 8 rouses everyone to take that first step.

# Time Motivation by Enneagram Type

Next we will explore time as a commodity. Each Enneagram type is motivated differently by time, which influences their behaviors and their sense of urgency or patience.

One way to frame this exploration is to think of time as either abundant or scarce. For those who are not necessarily motivated by time, it can appear abundant in relation to other factors. For those who are motivated by time, it can appear scarce and valuable.

Let's examine how time motivates each type, how it ranks in relation to other considerations, and whether each type is more motivated by perceived scarcity of time (urgency) or abundance (patience).

# Type 1 – Urgency
## Time Is Important, but Subordinate to "Getting It *Right*"

Type 1s are masterful at procrastination, putting things off for later. Some people may put off doing something important simply because they do not want to do it, but for the 1 that is not necessarily the case. The main reason Type 1s procrastinate is that they are daunted by how much time and energy they need to expend to complete the task to perfection. They set expectations for themselves so high that they dread starting a task, making them prone to procrastination. A person observing Type 1s may get the impression that the 1s feel they have an abundance of time because they appear to be in no hurry to start and seem less sensitive to deadlines than other types.

While the 1s procrastinate, they maintain an acute awareness of the impending deadline. The tipping point to action occurs when time becomes so scarce that their motivation to complete the task to their high standards compels them to get started. Once they start, they take on a frenetic sense of urgency, their apparent patience flipping to impatience as they work to finish the task.

Often, the 1s will not have left themselves enough time to complete the task by the deadline. Will the 1 submit an imperfect product? Not likely! For the 1, it is more important to get it right than to meet the deadline.

## Type 2 – Patience
## All the Time in the World to Help Out

Type 2s are driven much less by a consideration of time than they are by the desire to build emotional bonds and garner appreciation from others. The 2s will take all the time they need to help others in order to get that appreciation. In that way, the 2s treat time as an abundant commodity and not a top concern.

Type 2s are only motivated by time out of consideration for others and how it affects their ability to help. For the 2s, time in and of itself is not a big motivating factor. The intersection of their desire to help and their perception of time as being abundant makes the 2s one of the most patient types.

## Type 3 – Urgency
## Time Is Money

Type 3s appreciate the important role that time plays in achieving success, and money can be a common metric of success. As the saying goes, "Time is money."

The 3s are keenly aware that there are only so many minutes in a day, and they are highly motivated to make the most of each minute in achieving their goals. From this point of view, the 3 falls into the "time as scarce" camp, and they are eager to use every moment as effectively as possible. Because of this, Type 3s act with a sense of urgency and can often be impatient.

That said, being "on time" is not the highest priority for the 3s. Appearing successful is paramount to Type 3s, and they will take the time needed to make that impression, even if it makes them late.

On-time delivery is only important when it is a metric of success as seen by others in their community.

Furthermore, Type 3s will not let the amount of time it takes to get something done stand in the way of getting started, as Type 1s do. They want to get the task done as quickly and efficiently as possible so they can get onto the next task—the next opportunity to showcase their success.

The 3s also have the ability to "make time," so to speak. They are not daunted by how much energy they imagine it will take to get a task done. The 3s have tremendous energy, and they have no compunction about using it. If they need more time to get a task done, they will find that time by working late into the night if necessary—"making time" to reach their goal.

The 3s' ability to "make time" and "find time" could land them in the "time is abundant" camp as well. They rarely think that there is not enough time to finish a task. This ability enables the 3s to always have the time to accomplish their goals. As such, I put Type 3s in both camps—scarcity and abundance—yet always acting with a sense of urgency.

## Type 4 – Patience
## Time Is the Abundant Water
## in Which We All Swim

While Type 4s are reacting to their environment, their emotions envelop them. While the passage of time or a certain time of day may evoke a feeling in the 4, time in and of itself would not necessarily cause a reaction. Rather, time is like water in which the 4 swims. It permeates everything, making it abundant, like water in the sea.

A 4 can have conscious awareness of time, but time does not necessarily provide a motivating force. It can serve as a topic for philosophical or artistic consideration. They can revel in the way that time elicits emotions in themselves and others, and explore those emotions in art.

Because time is not a motivating force for the 4s, they tend to be more patient as they react to the world around them.

## Type 5 – Patience
## Time Is One of Many Considerations

If Type 4s appreciate the emotional impacts of time, Type 5s appreciate the logical ramifications of time. (Albert Einstein, likely a Type 5, theorized unconventional properties of time that he described in his special theory of relativity.) Type 5s will consider time carefully, along with everything else, as they go about their business of processing and categorizing information.

Curiously, Type 5s' appreciation of time does not necessarily translate into a motivating force on their behavior. Time is just one of many factors. Because of this, Type 5s tend to lack of a sense of urgency. The term "paralysis by analysis" illustrates the 5s' contentment with observing and analyzing the world without the need for action.

Although they have an explicit appreciation for time, Type 5s tend to consider it just one of many resources. And since they are not motivated by time, they tend to be patient. Also, if they consider time a valuable resource, they may be reluctant to give you any of theirs.

## Type 6 – Urgency
## Deadlines Increase Anxiety

The deadline looms. Will you finish in time? In contrast to the nonchalance of Type 5, Type 6 is acutely aware of time—a key component of anxiety for this type. Deadlines, whether self-imposed or from outside influences, increase the 6's anxiety.

Most 6s will tell you that when they wake up in the morning, they immediately start thinking about their to-do list for the day. As the day progresses, ticking things off the list lowers their anxiety.

A looming deadline increases anxiety, motivating the 6 to work that much harder to get things done. They feel that time is scarce and that there is never enough of it to accomplish everything. The anxiety caused by time also tends to make the 6s act with a sense of urgency. Type 6s are highly motivated by time.

## Type 7 – Urgency
## Never Enough Time to Have Fun

Type 7s are also in the Head-Thinking-Anxiety center and, as such, feel anxiety. Any unpleasantness associated with missing a deadline would compel the 7s to avoid that situation, especially if it reflects poorly on them. The 7s' anxiety arises mostly from fear that others would be unhappy or disappointed with them for failing to deliver on time, which prompts them to act with urgency to meet a deadline.

Anxiety from deadlines can also be self-imposed for the 7. Once relieved of the anxiety from external deadlines, the 7 will be anxious to get back to having fun. This keeps them in constant motion, acting with a sense of urgency.

## Type 8 – Urgency
## NOW, Let's Get It Done!

Type 8s want things done, and they want them done now. Once they have a goal in mind, they are motivated and impatient to get to work. From this point of view, they approach time as a scarce resource, wanting to minimize the amount of time spent accomplishing the goal.

Type 8s tend to be highly competitive, which is aligned with their sense of urgency and their desire to get things done quickly. They may use time as a competitive measuring stick, which makes time a key motivating factor for them.

## Type 9 – Patience
## Time for Harmony

Of all Enneagram types, Type 9s are arguably the best at appreciating every other type's perspectives. If you ask a 9 whether time is abundant or scarce, they put themselves in someone else's shoes and see how it can be both. Where would the 9s themselves fall?

Since Type 9s want to minimize conflict with and among those around them, they are motivated to consider everyone's opinions, concerns, and desires, and to ensure that everyone appreciates everyone else's perspectives. The 9 will take all the time necessary to make this happen, treating time as an abundant resource.

Those observing Type 9s would describe the 9s' behavior as patient and attentive. The 9s would not be compelled to action until there was a clear consensus that would avoid conflict. Curiously, the 9s themselves may be feeling impatient as they work to consider everyone's perspective and build the consensus. It is as if Type 9s are impatiently patient.

For the 9, working together in harmony is more important than meeting a deadline. Deadlines only become important when missing them causes conflict. The 9s are motivated more by avoiding the conflict than by a specific point in time represented by a deadline. Time itself is not a motivating factor for Type 9s, and they are arguably the most patient of all Enneagram types.

# Urgency and Patience in Problem Solving

Each Enneagram type considers the commodity of time as either abundant or scarce, which influences whether or not time serves as a motivating force. Those who treat time as scarce tend to have a strong sense of urgency while those who consider time abundant tend to be more patient. How do those tendencies play out during problem solving?

Step 1 – Urgency to right the wrong
Step 2 – Patience to build a team of stakeholders
Step 3 – Urgency to develop ideas for promising solutions
Step 4 – Patience as people react to the ideas
Step 5 – Patience to analyze the viability of each idea
Step 6 – Urgency to build a plan to reach the goal
Step 7 – Urgency to promote the plan
Step 8 – Urgency to implement the plan
Step 9 – Patience to integrate the solution with the community

Much like there is a need for different perspectives along the past-present-future timeline, there is also a need for urgency or patience at different times during problem solving. The Enneagram dynamics inform us as to which is important at each step.

Figure 6.4 illustrates how this sense of urgency or patience varies during the problem-solving process. The team cycles between urgency and patience in the beginning and ends with a strong sense of urgency during the highly active phases of Planning, Promotion, and Implementation (Steps 6, 7, and 8, respectively).

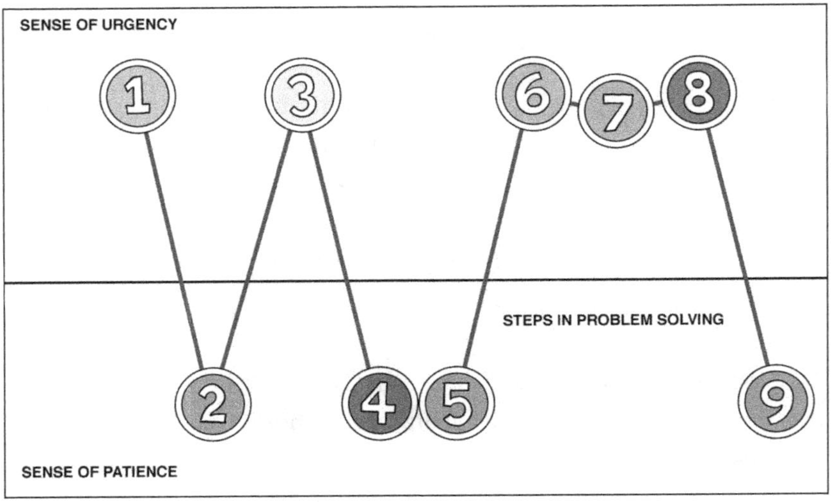

**Figure 6.4 – Urgency and Patience During Problem Solving**

Problem solving requires both a sense of urgency and a sense of patience, depending on which problem-solving step your team is addressing. It is important to value and appreciate both so your team can successfully navigate towards lasting solutions.

# Project Time: Being Present and Acting with Urgency in Step 8

Recalling the Enneagram problem-solving framework, project implementation does not kick off until Step 8 of the process—after a team has considered the seven preceding steps, either implicitly or explicitly (preferably explicitly).

The Implementation phase of the project exists in the time-space of the 8 dynamic, in the present and acting with *urgency*. For the sake of the following discussion, let's call this time-space *project time*.

Project execution in Step 8 requires a focus on getting the next thing done, meeting that next deadline. While the nature of Step 8 is that of Enneagram Type 8, the project team members are not necessarily all 8s (nor do you want them to be), so not all team members will share Type 8's project time motivation. How do you keep your project on schedule when your team includes types that are not motived by time or are not focused on the present? The answer lies in understanding, technique, and balance.

### Table 6.1 – Time Perspectives of Each Type

| Type | Urgency/Patience* | Timeline Focus Point |
|---|---|---|
| 1 | Urgency | Near Past |
| 2 | Patience | Distant Past |
| 3 | Urgency | Near Future |
| 4 | Patience | Present |
| 5 | Patience | Immediate Past |
| 6 | Urgency | Distant Future |
| 7 | Urgency | Immediate Future |
| 8 | Urgency | Present |
| 9 | Patience | Immediate Future |

*Urgency: motivated by time; patience: not motivated by time

# Tips for Project Managers

It is important for a project manager to appreciate each team member's perspective on time. Table 6.1 summarizes these perspectives. Ideally, all team members would have this understanding of and appreciation for themselves and their teammates.

With that understanding, you can develop strategies with your team members that enable them to contribute in ways that meet the scheduling demands of the project. This awareness will also alert you and your team to the pitfalls that can be avoided.

Each Enneagram type presents its own distinct challenges in the Implementation phase, Step 8 of problem solving. Based on our understanding of each type's time sensibility, let's explore techniques to keep them in *project time*—acting in the present and working with a sense of urgency towards the next project deliverable.

## Type 1 – Avoid the Reset Button

While Type 1s are motivated by time and can act with a sense of urgency, it is not the primary motivating factor. More important to the 1s is getting it right, where "right" is defined by a model that they have formulated in the past. In order to get it right, the 1s need to have all the information available, and they need it far enough in advance to have the time to process the information and perform the required task to their high standards.

Information and lead time are the key factors for the 1 to meet a deadline. Also, it is important not to change the information dramatically before the 1 has completed the task. Doing so is like hitting the reset button. As a leader, you need to be aware of this tendency of Type 1s and support them so that they have the information and time they need to complete their task to the standard at which they can feel satisfied.

## Special Tips for Working with a Type 1 to Meet a Deadline

If you are on a project with a deadline and you are counting on deliverables from colleagues who are Type 1s, here are some suggestions to help them deliver on time:

1) Have an open discussion about their tendency to work on tasks to perfection and discuss how that can take an extraordinary amount of time.

2) Share how valuable their contributions are to the team.

3) Remind them that meeting the deadline is also valuable.

4) Ask them what they need from you and others to complete the task by the deadline and help them get the information and resources they need as early as possible.

5) Encourage them to get started early. (How do you eat an elephant? *One bite at a time!*)

6) Type 1s often delay work, and any change to the information or circumstances can increase that tendency. Make sure that you provide the 1s with any new information as soon as possible. This way, you avoid hitting the reset button.

7) Check in with the 1s, but don't micromanage; they are already micromanaging themselves.

8) Avoid criticism, which reminds them that their work is imperfect and will likely cause delays.

## Type 2 – Never Too Much Appreciation

Type 2s are not motivated by time but by the desire to help and receive appreciation. If the 2s feel that they will be highly appreciated for delivering a task by a certain deadline, they will be highly motivated to receive that appreciation.

For Type 2s, the more appreciation, the better. I have not found a case where one can express too much appreciation for a 2. Generally, they can absorb all you can give. And the more frequently you express appreciation for the 2s, the more they are motivated to deliver. Keep up the stream of appreciation, and the 2s will stay on track.

## Type 3 – Ahead of Time

Type 3s rarely pose a challenge to the project in terms of on-time delivery. They are motivated by time and live in the near future. They will usually deliver their task early so they can move on to the next task, staying one step ahead.

## Type 4 – Now for Something Completely Different

Type 4s are less motivated by time than by being perceived as unique in some way. Inasmuch as the 4s can be recognized for their unique contributions to the project, they will move along their path of integration towards the energy of Type 1. Along this path, the 4 develops the self-motivation to complete tasks. Their reward is the acknowledgment for their unique contributions.

From my experience in the high-tech world, I have found that Type 4s are not drawn to roles on teams that operate continuously in project time, Step 8. Generally, the 4s have made their contributions much earlier in the process, before the Implementation phase starts. In Step 8 they may serve in consultative roles, advising the team on their earlier contributions.

If there is a Type 4 on your team during Step 8, the key to motivating them is to give them unique projects and recognize them for their novel contributions. Projects that require an understanding of the emotional reactions of others are ideal for the 4.

## Type 5 – Safe Space

Type 5s have access to the project time dynamic of Type 8 along their path of integration. If the 5s are allowed to master the information required to complete a task, they will do so confidently.

The 5s' reluctance to be proven wrong prevents them from making decisions when there is no clear right or wrong answer. They can spend a lot of time looking for a clear answer, even when no such answer exists. Also, the 5 will not be forthcoming with the fact that they are stuck.

As a leader, you need to be alert to this tendency in the 5 and assist in decision making, creating a safe space so that an incorrect decision does not reflect poorly on them. This will help the 5s continue to make progress towards the goal without getting stuck.

## Type 6 – Connecting the Dots

Type 6s are highly sensitive to time and motivated to complete tasks. Doing so lowers their anxiety. As long as they see a clear path to the final objective, the 6 will work doggedly on tasks that move the project towards that goal.

The mental energy for Type 6s is focused on the distant future. They need to see clearly how to connect the dots from the task at hand to the final goal. If the dots are not clear, or if there is any uncertainty, they will begin questioning whether it makes sense to do the task at all. As a leader, you need to be equipped to explain how the dots connect to the end goal in order to keep the 6 on track.

If the dots are not clear even to you, you can ask the 6 to trust you and keep plowing forward. That may work for a time, but it will become increasingly uncomfortable for the 6. Be ready when they return with more questions.

As a side note, I frequently find that Type 6s assume the role of project manager because it is their nature to map out tasks and connect the dots to project completion. The 6s are well equipped to do this as they see how all the pieces fit together in the big picture.

## Type 7 – Teamwork Time

Type 7s are focused on the immediate future and want to work on something fun. For the 7s, the more the merrier; generally, they want to interact with as many people as possible.

They are motivated by time inasmuch as they want to get to the next fun thing and/or avoid any unpleasantness. They pursue tasks that allow them to interact with others, and they do so with a sense of urgency. On the other hand, if Type 7s are given tedious tasks that do not interest them or allow them to interact with others, the tasks will languish.

As a leader, you need to understand this tendency in the 7s and direct them towards tasks that they can perform enthusiastically with others. Doing so will ensure the tasks are done on time since the 7s will not want to let down their teammates.

## Type 8 – Time to Conquer

Type 8s live in project time, acting in the present and looking forward to getting the task done. The key to ensuring that Type 8s stay on track is to give them the space to perform their tasks in a manner in which they feel in control. Type 8s don't like to be told what to do. It is better to clearly describe the goal to the 8, and let them figure out how to do it.

If the 8s ever feel challenged they will divert their energy towards facing the challenger rather than reaching the goal. The key is to make the goal the challenge so that the 8s focus their considerable energy on reaching that goal.

## Type 9 – Play Nice

The 9s are future focused—always alert to potential conflict on the project team. They are not motivated as much by time as by ensuring everyone is getting along harmoniously.

Should a conflict arise on the team, the 9s will divert their energy to resolving that conflict. This is great for the overall success of the project but may impact the 9s' ability to perform their specific tasks.

If you can create a conflict-free environment, the 9s will be less distracted and more able to focus on their assigned tasks. Because they do not want to be the source of conflict by not delivering on time, they will be compelled to finish their task by the deadline.

# A Preview of Work Team Triads

Another way to ensure teams are working with a sense of urgency is to group team members with complementary perspectives and motivations, selecting at least one teammate who is motivated by time. I have found that certain Enneagram types coalesce naturally into work teams. The combinations that work well together are commonly called Harmony triads: (1-4-7), (2-5-8), and (3-6-9). Chapter 7, "Work Team Triads: Two Balanced Brains," explores these work team groupings in detail; for now, let's examine each based on its collective sense of urgency.

Each group is composed of three people: one each from the intuitive center, the feeling center, and the thinking center. In these descriptions, I start with the intuitive center and show how the others complement it.

### Team 1-4-7

The 1 needs information and time to get a task done correctly, and the 7 wants to interact with people and avoid tedious work. Both are motivated by time but have other motivations that must be considered. When paired together, the 7 can perform the information collection work and the 1 can perform the tedious work of processing the details—work the 7 abhors. They work together in a complementary fashion, each leveraging their natural skills and tendencies.

When a Type 4 is added to the trio, the 1 and the 7 bring a sense of urgency while the 4 brings patience. Also, the 4 brings the focus to the present to complement the 7's future focus and the 1's past focus. The 4 is also sensitive to how others will respond emotionally to the team's work product.

## Team 2-5-8

When an 8 is paired with a 5, the 8 brings a sense of urgency and confident decision making that eludes the 5, allowing them as a team to make decisions on the information collected and analyzed by the 5. Adding Type 2 to the mix balances patience with the 8's urgency and provides a human connection to the team based on relationships.

## Team 3-6-9

When a 9, who is not motivated by time, is teamed with a 3 and a 6, the resulting team's future-biased sense of urgency will keep the group moving forward. This team is unique in that all members are future focused.

# Summary

The Enneagram provides a framework for understanding how people relate to time in two distinct ways. First, the Mental Energy Timeline illustrates where each Enneagram type tends to spend most of their mental energy—in the past, present, or future. Second, for each type, time itself serves as a motivating force to varying degrees, driving each type to act with patience or with a sense of urgency.

By understanding these relationships to time, you can better understand the role each Enneagram type plays on a project team and in problem solving. By employing techniques to align the motivating factors of each type with the goals of the project, you can keep your team members focused on moving towards those goals in a timely manner.

The Enneagram shows that each type brings unique perspectives on time and entreats us to value of having a diverse set of teammates and perspectives. By combining different types into small work teams, the different types can complement each other's perspectives to provide balanced working groups. In Chapter 7, "Work Team Triads: Two Balanced Brains," I delve further into the power of work groups and show how the work group dynamics are linked to brain function.

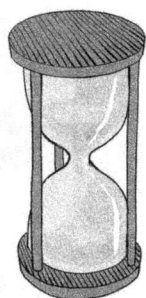

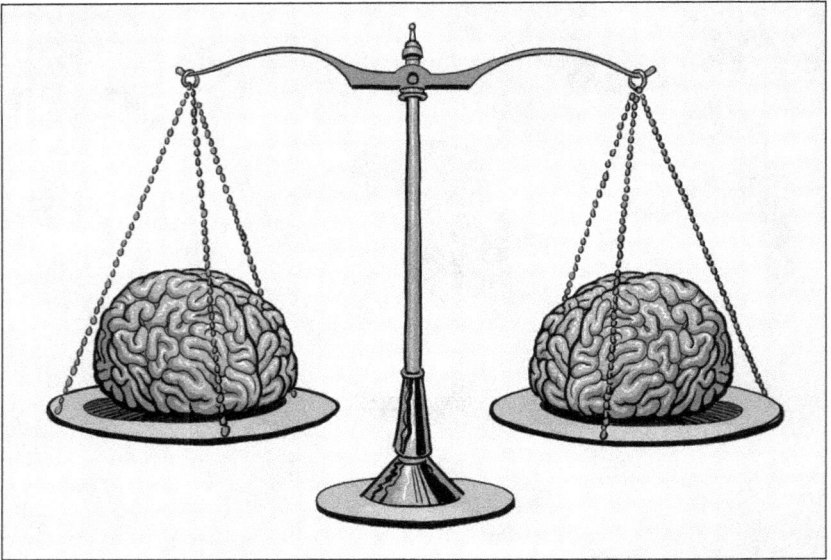

# Work Team Triads: Two Balanced Brains

After studying the Enneagram for several years, I became more convinced that there must be something hardwired in the structure of the human brain that manifests as the nine distinct Enneagram types. Being the skeptical Type 6 and trained in the scientific method, I tested and tested the Enneagram and continued to be impressed with how it held up to scrutiny and consistently predicted behaviors. The 6s are nothing if not lovers of consistency, and the Enneagram delivers.

I was determined to figure out the Brain-Enneagram connection and started searching for information that might lead me to an explanation. I soon stumbled upon a self-published book by Peter Savich titled *Personality and the Brain.*

Using medical journals and papers, Savich researched personality changes in patients that suffered brain damage, focusing on studies that described direct observations. Through his research, Savich was able to isolate the parts of the brain that govern the behaviors described by the Enneagram and develop a simple, elegant model that maps two brain structures to each of the nine Enneagram types. Wow!

I read Savich's book twice. After pondering his work, I contacted him. It turns out that he lives nearby. We became fast friends and have been working to develop his ideas ever since. We discuss and formulate experiments to prove his theory. I am very grateful to Peter for the effort he has put into his research and his book. I strongly recommend it to anyone interested in exploring the Brain-Enneagram connection more deeply.

In this chapter, I will summarize Savich's theory and show how it describes the main centers of the Enneagram: the intuitive center (8-9-1), the feeling center (2-3-4), and the thinking center (5-6-7).

Savich's theory also proposes a biological underpinning to the Temperament triads described in this chapter, often called the Assertive triad (3-7-8), the Compliant triad (1-2-6), and the Withdrawing triad (4-5-9), and which Savich calls Optimistic, Pessimistic, and Symmetrical, respectively.

After summarizing Savich's work, I will describe how I have applied his theory and my workplace observations to a third set of triads that I call the *work team triads*: (1-4-7), (2-5-8), and (3-6-9). I have found that the members of these triads often choose to work together since they have a natural affinity for one another. I will postulate a reason for this affinity using Savich's theory. Based on the nature of these teams in the workplace, I call them:

- Start Up triad (1-4-7)
- Industrious triad (2-5-8)
- Systematizing triad (3-6-9)

The work team triads each have a distinct leadership style and Mental Energy Timeline focus. I will demonstrate how these distinctions come into play during the problem-solving life cycle. Based on Savich's theory, I will show how the work team triads comprise two balanced brains.

# Savich's Theory

Savich hypothesizes that two parts of the brain uniquely differentiate the nine Enneagram types: the amygdala and the prefrontal cortex (PFC). For both structures, there is a right side and a left side. In the same way that each of us can be right-handed, left-handed, or ambidextrous, each of us can also have a PFC that is right-side dominant, left-side dominant, or symmetrically activate (dual). The same holds true for the amygdala.

Savich proposes that the three distinct modalities of the amygdala, when combined with the three modalities of the PFC, result in the nine types that make up the Enneagram.

# The Amygdala

The amygdala is a part of the brain found in vertebrates that plays a central role in responses to both threats and pleasure. It is a well-connected part of the brain, with predominantly outbound neural connections to other parts of the brain. When the amygdala is stimulated, it sends out signals and orchestrates a response to the stimulus. Here, I will focus on the amygdala's threat response since the resulting behaviors map clearly to the behaviors described by the Enneagram.

Because the human brain has two distinct hemispheres, we have two amygdalae—a right amygdala and a left amygdala. Certain research cited by Savich supports the view that the two amygdalae play different roles in our response to stimuli.

Savich sums up the implications of his research as follows:

- The right amygdala predominantly generates a subconscious fear response.
- The left amygdala predominantly informs consciousness as to the existence and level of fear.

If these implications are true, they are profound. They would mean that when the alarm signal from the left amygdala reaches consciousness, this signal would create fear awareness and trigger a "flight" response to a threat. On the other hand, the right amygdala signal, being subconscious, would be the source of the fear-unaware or "fight" response. In other words, if the subconscious response (right amygdala) were the stronger signal, the conscious mind would be fear unaware and would fight; if the left amygdala response were stronger, the fear would be more conscious and trigger a flight response.

Analogous to the brain dominances that drive right- and left-handedness, it follows that if people can be right amygdala dominant, they would tend to stand and fight while the left amygdala dominant people would be more inclined to flee. How do these tendencies map to the Enneagram? And what about the symmetrically active, dual amygdala types?

## The Amygdala-Enneagram Connection

Savich uses "aware fear" and "unaware fear" to describe the amygdala dominances where the left amygdala signal corresponds to the fear-aware (flight) response and the right amygdala signal corresponds to the fear-unaware (fight) response.

The behaviors dictated by the amygdalae's responses are increasingly well understood in neuroscience. Savich theorizes that the amygdalae responses correspond to the Enneagram's main triads. In Chapter 1, "The Enneagram Briefly," we saw that the Enneagram framework is divided into three groups of three types: the Gut-Intuitive-Anger center (8-9-1), the Heart-Feeling-Emotion center (2-3-4), and the Head-Thinking-Anxiety center (5-6-7). Savich describes how the main Enneagram triads represent our amygdala response to environmental stimulus. Let's examine this possibility.

## Response of the Gut-Intuitive-Anger Center

Savich's model asserts that the fear-unaware (fight) response corresponds to the Gut-Intuitive-Anger types of the Enneagram. Types 8, 9, and 1 are guided by an anger response to a threat stimulus in the environment. All three intuitive types work to eliminate the source of the stimulus; each has a unique strategy, but all three strategies involve directly confronting the source of the stimulus. Where the left amygdala dominant, fear-aware types consciously feel fear or anxiety, the right amygdala dominant, fear-unaware types experience anger.

Of the nine Enneagram types, Type 8 most stereotypically represents the "fight" response, usually by directly confronting the threat stimulus. Type 9 also seeks to eliminate the source of the threat, generally by employing an appeasement or passive-aggressive strategy. Type 1 frames threats in terms of right and wrong and unwaveringly fights to eliminate the wrongs. In each case, the fear-unaware response enables each of these types to directly confront the threat. Savich hypothesizes that the Enneagram's Gut-Intuitive-Anger center corresponds to right amygdala dominance in these three types.

## Response of the Head-Thinking-Anxiety Center

What does the Enneagram say about the amygdala's flight response? The Head-Thinking-Anxiety types (5, 6, and 7) are the best candidates for those with left amygdala dominance. These are the fear-aware folks—those who are most aware of fear when faced with a threat in their environment. While under threat, all three types experience an increase in anxiety that compels a flight response.

In response, Type 5 retreats to the safety of their "castle," their safe place away from the threat. Type 7 also tries to quit an uncomfortable situation that makes them feel unsafe by seeking alternatives that are fun and fear-free. The 6 experiences an acute increase in anxiety when faced with a threat.

Curiously, the 6 can respond in either of two ways: the phobic response or the counterphobic response. The 6 in phobic response seeks the protection of trusted authorities or systems. The 6 in counterphobic response suppresses anxiety to the point that they confront the threat directly, even if it is unsafe for them to do so.

For all three Head-Thinking-Anxiety types, their response is driven by the sense of anxiety and fear awareness, exactly the response that appears to be orchestrated by the left amygdala.

## Response of the Heart-Feeling-Emotion Center

If the intuitive center corresponds to a dominant right amygdala, and the thinking center corresponds to a dominant left amygdala, what about the feeling center (2-3-4)? While the first two groups can be understood by a dominance of the right or left amygdala, respectively, the Heart-Feeling-Emotion center can be best understood by activation of both amygdalae.

The feeling center types are not driven by an obvious anger response or an obvious anxiety response. The combined response of the two amygdalae appears to lead to an emotional awareness that allows these types to have a nuanced understanding of their feelings without being overwhelmed by either anger or fear. This symmetrical response allows the feeling types to engage with the threat stimulus. Rather than try to destroy the stimulus or flee from it, their response compels them to interact with it.

Type 2 seeks to build an emotional bond by helping, Type 4 communicates at a viscerally emotional level, and Type 3 seeks to determine what defines success and strives to achieve that success. Each type relies on communication as the tool to address the stimulus. The word that Savich uses for this interaction is "negotiation." This balanced, emotion-based approach is typical of those with dual amygdalae activations.

I find it fascinating that the three possible activations (right, left, and dual) of one of the oldest parts of the brain—a structure found in all vertebrates—correspond perfectly to the three centers of the Enneagram. Even though it is only in the last few decades that science has given us insight into the neurobiological function of the amygdalae, the behaviors governed by the amygdalae have been discernable to anyone paying attention since the beginning of humankind. Fundamentally, the Enneagram framework appears to describe behaviors attributed to amygdala dominances.

## Prefrontal Cortex

Savich calls the PFC the optimism/pessimism processor. I also call it the glass-half-full/glass-half-empty processor. Like the amygdala, the PFC has two possible dominances: left and right. The optimistic, glass-half-full processing generally occurs in the left side, and the pessimistic, glass-half-empty processing occurs in the right side. Each of us can be left-dominant PFC, right-dominant PFC, or symmetrically active, dual PFC.

If they see a nut up in a tree, the glass-half-full types are inclined to think, "I am going to climb that tree and enjoy that nut." If the glass-half-empty types see that same nut, they are inclined to think, "If I climb that tree I may fall and break my leg." The dual PFC type will fall in the middle, likely going along with the consensus of those around them.

Savich's research uncovered that PFC functionality overlaps with other triads described by the Enneagram: the Temperament or Hornevian triads, (3-7-8), (1-2-6), and (4-5-9). Savich theorizes that the (3-7-8) triad corresponds to more optimistic glass-half-full types, (1-2-6) corresponds to more pessimistic glass-half-empty types, and (4-5-9) corresponds to dual PFC types who fall somewhere in between.

Karen Horney (1885–1952) is often attributed with identifying and describing the Temperament triads (see Table 7.1). She was a neo-Freudian psychoanalyst and used words to describe the Temperament triads based on the terminology of that time.

I have some issues with this wording in the context of Savich's work. Certainly, Types 3, 7, and 8 tend to be assertive, but I do not consider Type 1 to be "compliant." Likewise, I would not characterize Type 4 as "withdrawing." Alternatively, if we lean on Savich's descriptions, the triad labels become Optimistic, Pessimistic, and Symmetrical.

### Table 7.1 – Temperament Triads

| Triad | Hornevian Labels | Savich Labels |
|-------|------------------|---------------|
| 3-7-8 | Assertive | Optimistic |
| 1-2-6 | Compliant | Pessimistic |
| 4-5-9 | Withdrawing | Symmetrical |

I believe that these are better descriptors and draw on the specific link to the PFC. I realize that the pessimistic types, like myself, often object to being called pessimistic (especially in the US), preferring "realistic" or some other descriptor. I offer my apologies to the 1s, 2s, and 6s.

Table 7.2 summarizes the relationships between the Enneagram types and the dominances of the amygdala and PFC. Savich derives from scientific papers on neuroscience to theorize how each dominance of the amygdala and PFC governs certain behaviors, and he connects the dots between those behaviors and Enneagram types. In doing so, he formulates a simple, elegant model that maps brain function to the Enneagram.

To my knowledge, this model has not yet been thoroughly tested, but it holds promise as the underlying neurobiological foundation for the Enneagram. In the next section, we take this theory one step further and look at its implications for teamwork.

**Table 7.2 – Enneagram Types and Brain Structure Dominances**

| Enneagram Type | Amygdala Dominance | Amygdala Mental Bias | PFC Dominance | PFC Mental Bias |
|---|---|---|---|---|
| 1 | Right | Fear unaware | Right | Pessimistic |
| 2 | Dual | Symmetrical | Right | Pessimistic |
| 3 | Dual | Symmetrical | Left | Optimistic |
| 4 | Dual | Symmetrical | Dual | Symmetrical |
| 5 | Left | Fear aware | Dual | Symmetrical |
| 6 | Left | Fear aware | Right | Pessimistic |
| 7 | Left | Fear aware | Left | Optimistic |
| 8 | Right | Fear unaware | Left | Optimistic |
| 9 | Right | Fear unaware | Dual | Symmetrical |

Source: Peter Savich, "The Enneagram and Patterns of Asymmetric Dominance in Orbitofrontal Cortex and Amygdala," December 2007 (personalityandthebrain.org/paper.htm).

# Work Team Triads

Savich's work resulted in a provocative hypothesis. Assuming his theory is true, it has some dramatic implications for work teams. The Enneagram describes a third set of triads—(1-4-7), (2-5-8), and (3-6-9)—which are referred to as the Harmony triads in Enneagram literature. For example, Dr. David Daniels describes these triads on his website.

In the workplace, I have observed that the Harmony triad types often coalesce into work teams. They tend to have an affinity for one another and work well together. Because of this affinity, I call these triads the *work team triads* and will refer to them as such hereafter. I call the (1-4-7) triad the Start Up triad, the (2-5-8) triad the Industrious triad, and the (3-6-9) triad the Systematizing triad.

Why do these particular triads work so well together? Referring back to Savich's theory, I noticed that the work team triads have a perfect balance of amygdala and PFC dominances.

## Two Balanced Brains

Table 7.3 shows that the three types comprising each of the work team triads balance both amygdala and PFC activations, with one each of left-dominant, right-dominant, and symmetrically active (dual). In other words, when the members of the work team triads form a three-person team, collectively they comprise two balanced brains from the perspective of amygdala and PFC dominances. In terms of the Enneagram, these teams include one representative from each of the main centers and one from each of the Temperament triads.

## Table 7.3 – Work Team Triads

| Type | Amygdala | PFC | Main Centers | Temperament Triads |
|---|---|---|---|---|
| **Start Up Triad** | | | | |
| 1 | Right | Right | Intuitive | Pessimist |
| 4 | Dual | Dual | Feeling | Symmetrical |
| 7 | Left | Left | Thinking | Optimist |
| **Industrious Triad** | | | | |
| 2 | Dual | Right | Feeling | Pessimist |
| 5 | Left | Dual | Thinking | Symmetrical |
| 8 | Right | Left | Intuitive | Optimist |
| **Systematizing Triad** | | | | |
| 3 | Dual | Left | Feeling | Optimist |
| 6 | Left | Right | Thinking | Pessimist |
| 9 | Right | Dual | Intuitive | Symmetrical |

Notice that each of the work team triads forms a triangle within the Enneagram diagram. You can move from one triad to the next by rotating that triangle like a dial clockwise from (1-4-7) to (2-5-8) to (3-6-9). Let's start with the (1-4-7) triad and consider how each work team triad delivers its distinctive style.

## Start Up Triad (1-4-7)

Dr. Daniels calls the (1-4-7) triad the "Idealists Triad," likely because the idealistic Type 1 connects to both the 4 and the 7 along the path of integration of the 4 and the path of disintegration of the 7. This group is tuned for right-wrong thinking, which gives it the characteristic of idealism.

I find that this particular triad is adept at performing innovative work. The 1, 4, and 7 provide all the necessary ingredients for developing new concepts. The 1 provides the initial impetus by identifying a wrong that needs to be righted. The 4 has the unique ability to see what is missing and convey that missing piece in an emotionally impactful way. The 7 provides the enthusiasm and networking that feed the 1 and the 4 with both energy and new ideas. This combination of types is ideally suited to tackle challenges for which there is no obvious solution.

Living in Silicon Valley and observing start-up companies over the years, I have noticed that the founding teams often comprise some combination of Types 1, 4, and 7. Anecdotally, it is either the 4 or the 7 that serves as the energy to found the company. They are often the serial entrepreneurs that are so prevalent here.

Intriguingly, whether a company is founded by a 4 or a 7, the founder will often choose a 1 to manage operations. During the start-up phase, a company may change directions several times, which requires a team that is both adaptable and creative as they endeavor to identify the combination of products and business models that will prove successful. The (1-4-7) team delivers this powerful combination during the nascent phase of a product, a project, or a company.

## Industrious Triad (2-5-8)

Turning the dial one click clockwise takes you to the (2-5-8) triad. Dr. Daniels refers to this group as the "Relationists Triad" since much of the drive for each of these three types derives from their relation to those around them. I find that teams composed of these types often take on operational roles in an organization. The core for this triad is the 8, connected to both the 2 and the 5 through their paths of integration and disintegration, respectively.

The 8 drives this group with the constant call to action. The 8 is living in the here and now, responding to the immediate situation, overcoming obstacles, and getting the job done. The 8 works well with both the 2 and the 5, with the 2 providing helpful energy to support the team and the 5 providing information and insights to keep the team on track. Based on the operational focus of this particular triad, my preferred description is the Industrious triad.

## Systematizing Triad (3-6-9)

Rotating the dial to the third position brings us to the (3-6-9) Systematizing triad. Unlike the other work team triads, the (3-6-9) triad does not have an obvious middle or core type since all three are connected to one another through their paths of integration and disintegration. This may be a clue to the nature of this work team.

Enneagram Type 9 devotes much energy to understanding the perspectives of others. Because this triad comprises the three core types of the main Enneagram centers (9-Intutive, 3-Feeling, and 6-Thinking), it may, by its very composition, be the triad best able to appreciate and represent all other types. In this way, I think that the 9 serves as the core type for the Systematizing triad. This is borne out by the fact that the 9 is from the Gut-Intuitive-Anger center, like the core types (1 and 8) of the other two work team triads.

As core types, each type in this triad represents the suppressed state of their center. And while the suppression of emotion, anxiety, and anger for the 3, 6, and 9, respectively, may pose a challenge for any one of the types individually, working as a team they complement one another and provide visibility in each other's blind spots.

Assuming that Type 9 serves as the core for the (3-6-9) Systematizing triad, I look to the roles that Type 9s play in organizations. The 9s typically migrate to service roles. For instance, there is no better type than the 9 to serve in the role of customer service for your organization. The 9 is also well suited for service roles such as IT, project management, and leadership positions.

In each of these service roles, you will find that 3s, 6s, and 9s all perform particularly well. As a work team, they will endeavor to optimize for success (3 dynamic) while minimizing risk (6 dynamic) and minimizing conflict (9 dynamic). This team is highly attentive to the needs and issues of others, and they all strive in their respective ways to maintain harmony, solve problems, and enable their teams to work together as effectively as possible. These characteristics are consistent with Dr. Daniels's label of the "Pragmatists Triad." This triad achieves these aims by thinking about the way people work together and putting into place systems, processes, and work flows that ensure work gets done efficiently. That is why I call this group the Systematizing triad.

## One Balanced Brain

While the work team triads collectively comprise two balanced brains, there are pairs of Enneagram types that together comprise one balanced brain for amygdala and PFC:

- Type 1 (Fear Unaware, Pessimistic) and Type 7 (Fear Aware, Optimistic)
- Type 6 (Fear Aware, Pessimistic) and Type 8 (Fear Unaware, Optimistic)

Curiously, I find that these pairs will often come together as married couples.

Also, there is one type that has a completely balanced brain all to themselves. That is Type 4, with balanced amygdala and balanced PFC. Of all types, Type 4 may have the best vantage point to understand all other types. Perhaps this is why they can speak to all of us through their art.

# Problem Solving with the Work Team Triads

In each of the work team triads, the different Enneagram types contribute distinct problem-solving talents. Let's examine these talents and explore how the three types complement each other to form effective problem-solving teams.

## Problem Solving: Start Up Triad (1-4-7)

The Start Up triad (1-4-7), with Type 1 at its core, will be the first to identify a wrong in the world and have the burning desire to correct it. There will be a sense of finding beauty and justice, all the while riding the coattails of the 7's optimistic energy. While the team will expect the 7 to take a leadership role, the 4 may provide more of the actual direction for the group.

Here is how I see this team working: The 1 will ground the team on the problem that needs to be solved, the wrong that needs to be righted. Ideas will come from all the members of this triad—the 1 sees how things "should" be, the 4 sees what is missing, and the 7 serves as the idea pollinator.

When a new idea comes to the team, the 4 will have the most intense emotional reactions to it, which can serve as a filtering mechanism. Once an idea makes it through the 4's emotional gauntlet, the 1 will analyze the idea to ensure that it solves the problem perfectly. Should the idea look promising to the 7, the optimistic enthusiasm will kick in and pull the team forward to muster the resources necessary to solve the problem. As you can see, these roles are highly complementary. The Start Up triad works together effectively, appreciating each other's contributions and moving forward with minimal conflict.

## Problem Solving:
## Industrious Triad (2-5-8)

Speaking of conflict, let's examine the Industrious triad. The core dynamic of this triad lies in the energy of the 8, starting to act. To be compelled to action means that a problem will already have been identified and an idea to solve that problem proposed. At that point, the problem-solving process becomes operational. How do the Industrious triad types work together?

Consider this hypothetical situation: The 2 knows someone with a problem and feels compelled to help. The relationship between the 2 and the 8 motivates the 8 to get involved to solve the problem. (The 8 knows that they can fix it and that everyone else is just complaining and not getting anything done, which frustrates the 8.) The 8 would have a sense of the direction to take and would start moving the team in that direction.

Behind the scenes, the 5 would be thinking about the proposed solution to the problem by analyzing it and thinking of pros and cons. If the 5 identifies a possible obstacle, they would communicate that to the team objectively. If the 8 perceives the obstacle as a threat to the plan, then their first reaction might be to argue or dismiss it.

Rather than being frustrated, the 5 finds the 8's behavior amusing, so there is little conflict between them. The 2 generates an idea for a new direction and continues helping in order to receive appreciation from the 5 and 8, which they generously give. This allows the team to move forward, working together to implement a solution that solves the problem.

## Type 8 Leaders and the 24-Hour Rule

A Type 5 who worked on a team dominated by a Type 8 leader once shared a technique he used to communicate with the 8. Being the thoughtful, analytical type, the 5 would often have thought through the consequences of a course of action and would know that it would hit a dead end. Knowing that there was no point in discussing or arguing the point with the 8 leader, the 5 would simply, out of the blue, mention the inevitable outcome of the current direction, and then shut up. He noticed that nothing would happen right away, but usually within 24 hours, the 8 would have a sudden change of mind and head the team in a new direction. There would never be an acknowledgment of a mistake or even that the impetus for the new direction had come from the 5. The 5 had figured out how to communicate with the 8 so that his thought became the 8's idea for a new direction, thereby averting problems foreseen by the 5.

## Problem Solving: Systematizing Triad (3-6-9)

Now let's turn to the Systematizing triad. The core dynamic of this triad is Type 9, which strives to reduce conflict. The types of problems that this triad seeks to solve involve the resolution of any conflicts in the environment. As you can imagine, when there is a conflict, emotions will run high—except for one type.

The gift of Type 3 is their suppressed emotional response. Even in an emotionally charged situation, Type 3s can assess the situation in an emotionally neutral manner. This allows them to objectively arrive at ideas for solutions without imposing their own emotional baggage on any idea. To the 3, the main imperative is pursuing ideas that are likely to succeed.

Because Type 3 suppresses their own emotional reactions, they will not have a strong sense for how other people will react to their ideas. Fortunately, both the 6 and the 9 have a much better sense of how people might react. The 6 (representing the Head-Thinking-Anxiety center) will be able to sense how anxious an idea will make people feel. The 9 (representing the Gut-Intuitive-Anger center) will intuitively know how much disagreement a proposal will generate.

By running the 3's ideas through the anxiety and anger filters of the 6 and 9, the Systematizing triad can generate proposals that are likely to succeed while minimizing both risk (anxiety) and conflict (anger). With a promising idea in hand, the 6 will be compelled to map out a plan to implement the solution. Once the plan is completed, the 3 will want to get to work implementing the solution and the 9 will remain alert to ensure that the project integrates well within the community. Each type complements the others and serves the team, enabling them to implement solutions that work harmoniously with the community and the environment.

## Work Team Triads and Time

Though each work team triad provides access to the full range of amygdala and PFC dominances, they each have their own unique approach. Next, let's examine each triad in relation to the time sensibilities we explored in Chapter 6, "The Enneagram and Time."

Table 7.4 summarizes the Mental Energy Timeline focus and urgency or patience of each Enneagram type, organized by work team triads. In terms of time motivation, we see that each triad has at least one type that acts with urgency and one that acts with patience.

## Table 7.4 – Work Team Triads and Time

| Type | Urgency or Patience | Mental Energy Timeline |
|---|---|---|
| **Start Up Triad** | | |
| 1 (core) | Urgency | Past |
| 4 | Patience | Present |
| 7 | Urgency | Future |
| **Industrious Triad** | | |
| 2 | Patience | Past |
| 5 | Patience | Past |
| 8 (core) | Urgency | Present |
| **Systematizing Triad** | | |
| 3 | Urgency | Future |
| 6 | Urgency | Future |
| 9 (core) | Patience | Future |

The Start Up triad has one each of past, present, and future, with the core Type 1 focused on the past. The Industrious triad types focus on both present and past, with the core Type 8 focusing on the present. Strikingly, the Systematizing triad is entirely focused on the future, including the core Type 9.

As we rotate the dial through each work team triad—from Start Up to Industrious to Systematizing—we are in effect moving the work team focus from the past to the present, and then to the future. I call this the *starting point* in time for each of the work team triads.

Since the relevance of time is so important to the nature of each work team triad and its relationship to problem solving, the following section explores these relationships in depth.

Also, consider how the starting point—past, present, or future—applies not just to work teams but to any organization and its lifecycle phase—early, growing, or mature.

 — Past

## Start Up Triad (1-4-7) – Starting Point: Past

We have examined how Type 1—the core of the Start Up triad—refers to the past to formulate models of right and wrong to construct their ideological framework. These references to the past serve as the foundation for identifying and characterizing the problems that the Start Up triad will tackle. They also serve as a basis for assessing the viability of various solutions.

The 4 brings the Start Up triad into the present, providing insight into how stakeholders might react to ideas and proposals. The Type 4 dynamic ensures that the team pays attention and spends time in the present, not dwelling on the problem (1 dynamic) or daydreaming about the future (7 dynamic). The 4 can react (emotionally) to how proposals will solve the challenges people currently face.

The 7 is bored easily and is drawn to thinking about the future. They can home in on interesting proposals to which the 4 has reacted positively and will know instinctively which will be the most fun to pursue. Inasmuch as the 7's direction is consistent with the principles of the 1, the 1 will feel compelled to continue moving in that direction. In this way, past, present, and future all serve the team in its mission—moving beyond Type 1's starting point in the past.

The Start Up triad's combination of past, present, and future perspectives is ideal for a team tackling problems that have never been addressed: the 1 provides a past perspective (what big problem is unsolved), the 7 provides a future outlook (what the world will look like when we solve it), and the 4 conveys the present moment (how people react).

Present

## Industrious Triad (2-5-8) – Starting Point: Present

The Industrious triad's core Type 8 compels this triad to action in the present. While the Start Up triad is tuned to identifying a problem and devising a solution, the Industrious triad wants to take a solution and implement it.

The 8 is a natural leader and would likely serve in a leadership role on this team. While the 2 does not share the 8's sense of urgency, they are motivated to help the 8. The 2 will contribute energy to the team as long as the 8 feeds them ample appreciation. The 8 is straightforward and forthright, so the 2 will get immediate feedback, which will keep the 2 in sync with the 8 and on track to fulfill the 8's wishes.

The 2's relationships and anecdotes will inform the team, keeping them connected to the community and helping them avoid past mistakes. While the 8 compels the team to act in the present, the 2 provides important perspectives from the past.

Type 5s will react to and ruminate on information they receive from their teammates. Since the 5 is not motivated by a sense of urgency, they're in no hurry to produce results. Trying to motivate a 5 using deadlines is futile.

Fortunately for this team, the 8 is highly motivated by time and knows how to compel the 5 to act. Quite simply, the 8 can play on the 5's desire to appear competent; knowing that the 8 has no compunction about using humiliation as a tool keeps the 5 on track and contributing. The 5's ability to analyze vast amounts of information keeps the project team informed and helps them avoid pitfalls.

The Industrious triad is perfectly tuned to producing results quickly (Type 8), balanced by the desire to maintain good relationships (Type 2) and appear competent (Type 5).

## Fail Fast

In Silicon Valley, we are constantly exploring different styles of product development. One of the currently popular methodologies is called Agile. Part of the Agile method—a technique called Fail Fast—is aligned with the work style of the Industrious triad.

Using the Fail Fast technique, a team tries an idea based on its intuition (Type 8 dynamic), its experience (Type 2 dynamic), and a best guess based on the current information (Type 5 dynamic), and proceeds quickly (Type 8 dynamic) to see if the idea works. If it does, great! If it doesn't, adjust and try again. These dynamics reflect the style of the Industrious triad.

Fail Fast serves well for solving certain categories of problems, especially where the cost of failure is low. When the cost of failure is high, it is better to use a technique with a deliberate look into the future, including the implications, ramifications, and consequences of failure—as represented by the Type 6 dynamic. The Systematizing triad brings this perspective.

The Fail Fast technique may be deliberate, or it may arise from the team composition. Chapter 8, "Team Diagnostics Toolbox," includes a detailed analysis of an accidental Fail Fast team, including strategies for balancing the dynamics.

Future

## Systematizing Triad (3-6-9) – Starting Point: Future

Type 9 lies at the core of the Systematizing triad. Curiously, this is the only work team triad that at its core is *not* motivated by time. Rather, it is motivated by anticipating and mitigating future conflicts.

While the 9 is highly tuned to prevent the next conflict, the 3 can look one step beyond that and envision a successful overall outcome. The 6 then has the ability to look even further into the future, mitigate risks, and invent systems that predictably and consistently realize the successful vision of the future.

The Systematizing triad derives its sense of urgency from both the 3 and the 6. The 6 feels the anxiety of impending risks and urgently works to quell that anxiety. The 3 is highly motivated to achieve successful outcomes and be recognized for that success as soon as possible. This makes the Systematizing triad a future-oriented team.

The Systematizing triad is perfectly tuned to building repeatable successful outcomes that deliver customer delight—a hallmark of a mature organization.

# Summary

Underlying all human activity is the human brain. Any model that represents human behavioral dynamics should have its basis in neuroscience. Savich has proposed a model that, while still theoretical, provides a convincing way to map Enneagram dynamics directly to amygdala and PFC functionality. This theory may explain how teams form and focus on certain types of problems.

Just as each Enneagram dynamic plays a distinct role in problem solving, each work team triad has a unique character and serves a different purpose. The cycles of problem solving can be applied to project teams, companies, and even countries and economies—any system based on human behavior.

CHAPTER 8

# Team Diagnostics Toolbox

Your team is stuck. No progress is being made. Are they complaining about the problems but not starting to solve them? Conversely, is everyone working furiously but making no progress towards the goal? Can't make a decision? Can't get attention from management for resources?

Your team's strengths and weaknesses will vary depending on the types of people on it. By using the concepts described in previous chapters—time sensibility and brain dominance—as diagnostic tools, you can tune your team for best performance. Additionally, you can use the type concentration analysis, or team wheel analysis, described in this chapter, to keep your team's problem-solving capabilities at their best and your team rolling forward towards its objective.

## The Team Wheel

The team wheel represents the concentration of Enneagram types on your problem-solving team. Ideally, your team is balanced for problem solving with neither over- or underrepresentation in any step in the problem-solving process. Realistically, that will not be the case. Even if your team has exactly nine people, the likelihood of there being exactly one of each Enneagram type is 1 in 9×9×9×9×9×9×9×9×9, or 1 in 387,420,489, which does not include larger or smaller teams. The bottom line is that most teams are imbalanced and will naturally get stuck. These tools will help you understand your team and compensate for imbalances in order to keep the team working together well.

## Overinflation, Underinflation, and Flats in Your Team Wheel

Your problem-solving journey can get bumpy if your team wheel is out of balance with either overrepresentation of an Enneagram type—over-inflation—or underrepresentation of a type—underinflation (a flat).

A team with members composed of predominantly one Enneagram type will be drawn to their particular strength or step in the problem-solving process and will be less inclined to engage in many of the other steps—especially the next step. For instance, a team overinflated with Type 4s would be very interested in examining the feelings and emotional reactions of stakeholders but reluctant to move into Step 5, which demands detailed logical analysis detached from feelings.

Another overinflation situation arises when someone on the team has a particularly dominant personality. That person may draw the team towards their Enneagram dynamic, downplaying the other problem-solving dynamics. A similar imbalance arises when your company culture has a particularly strong dominance. For instance, if your company has a Type 1 Perfectionist culture, then the team will be drawn towards Step 1 no matter where they are in the problem-solving process.

Underinflation can also slow your team's progress. For instance, imagine a team who has made it all the way through Step 7 in problem solving, but there is no action-oriented Type 8 energy on the team—no one who will fearlessly jump into action. The team may languish at this point and may even revert to discussing problems (Type 1 energy), like the problem that no one ever takes initiative!

Overinflation or underinflation—in either case your team will struggle. Using the team wheel as a diagnostic tool, you can help your team understand why they get stuck and how they can get rolling again.

## Steps in Diagnosing Your Team

When analyzing your team, you will want to determine the Enneagram types of each team member. There are many tools and tests available for this. For instance, I provide a questionnaire at www. EnneaSurvey.com. Once you have determined the likely type of each team member, assess how these types are distributed among the steps along the perimeter of the team wheel. Is each type on the wheel represented? Do you have a strong concentration of any one dynamic? These concentrations and deficiencies will give you clues as to where your team will excel and where it will struggle. It will also tell you where your team may get stuck and which steps the team may try to minimize or skip altogether.

Using the Mental Energy Timeline, look at the concentrations of types and determine whether they are predominantly focused on the future, the past, or the present. It will be necessary to cultivate all timeline perspectives within the team, especially as you generate and assess ideas. You do not want to dwell too long on either the future or the past. The balanced team will have a slight overall inclination towards the future.

Also examine your team's sense of urgency. Looking at the concentrations of the types on your team, what overall level of urgency is your team likely to feel? You will want to avoid moving too quickly or too slowly, which will depend in part on the overall sense of urgency. A team with too little urgency may have trouble moving from step to step in the process while a team with too much urgency may try to skip steps. The balanced team will have a slight inclination towards a sense of urgency.

Finally, using the mapping of brain dominances to Enneagram types we discussed in Chapter 7, "Work Team Triads: Two Balanced Brains," on page 201, determine the overall Enneagram type of your team. This is another way to understand the step or steps at which your team will excel and in which they will languish or attempt to skip. It will also suggest the Enneagram types you may want to add to your team to achieve balance.

For example, if your overall team type is Type 1, then you may want to include other types on the team to balance that out. Remember, the balanced team will have an equal distribution of dominances of both amygdala and PFC, including a balance of right, left, and dual dominances.

## The Balanced Team

While the likelihood of having a perfectly balanced team is exceedingly small, it is still a helpful baseline. Let's use the tools and examine the perfectly balanced team—a team that has one member of each type. What do the tools say about this team?

**Table 8.1 – Type Distribution Analysis of Ideally Balanced Team**

| Enneagram Type | No. of Team Members | Wheel Inflation |
|---|---|---|
| 1 | 1 | OK |
| 2 | 1 | OK |
| 3 | 1 | OK |
| 4 | 1 | OK |
| 5 | 1 | OK |
| 6 | 1 | OK |
| 7 | 1 | OK |
| 8 | 1 | OK |
| 9 | 1 | OK |
| **Total** | | |
| Members | 9 | |

Table 8.1 illustrates the balanced team of nine members with one member of each type. Such a team can form a perfectly balanced team wheel. I say "can" because we should not discount the possibility of a particularly strong personality introducing a dominant dynamic in their own Enneagram type. Still, the likelihood of any one personality dominating over all others is diminished—a nice feature of larger groups.

Table 8.2 shows this team's PFC and amygdala dominances. This ideally balanced team has equal representation of all parts of the brain that influence the Enneagram dynamics.

## Table 8.2 – Brain Dominance Analysis of Ideally Balanced Team

| Enneagram Type | No. of Team Members | PFC Dominance | PFC Weighting | Amygdala Dominance | Amygdala Weighting |
|---|---|---|---|---|---|
| 1 | 1 | Pessimistic | +1 | Fear unaware | +1 |
| 2 | 1 | Pessimistic | +1 | Dual | +1 |
| 3 | 1 | Optimistic | +1 | Dual | +1 |
| 4 | 1 | Dual | +1 | Dual | +1 |
| 5 | 1 | Dual | +1 | Fear aware | +1 |
| 6 | 1 | Pessimistic | +1 | Fear aware | +1 |
| 7 | 1 | Optimistic | +1 | Fear aware | +1 |
| 8 | 1 | Optimistic | +1 | Fear unaware | +1 |
| 9 | 1 | Dual | +1 | Fear unaware | +1 |
| | **Total** | | **Total** | | **Total** |
| Members | 9 | Pessimistic | +3 | Fear unaware | +3 |
| | | Optimistic | +3 | Fear aware | +3 |
| | | Dual | +3 | Dual | +3 |

Examining teams from the perspective of brain dominances gives additional insight into the missing ingredients of imbalanced teams. The work team triads showed us how the balance of brain dominances leads to cooperative teams with reduced discord. Extending that concept to larger teams, the composition of brain dominances gives us insight into how well we can expect our team to cooperate and how to adjust team membership to achieve a balance of all brain dominances.

Table 8.3 examines the time dimensions of the balanced team. All points on the timeline are represented, and there is a slight forward-looking bias. When we score tendencies towards urgency (+1) or patience (-1), the sum is +1. It makes sense that the balanced team would have both a slight inclination towards being focused on the future and a slight overall sense of urgency towards action. On a philosophical note, these inclinations towards the future and urgency may explain in part the underlying forces in human advancement.

### Table 8.3 – Time Analysis of Ideally Balanced Team

| Enneagram Type | No. of Team Members | Mental Energy Timeline | Timeline Weighting | Sense of Urgency/ Patience | Urgency/ Patience Weighting |
|:---:|:---:|:---:|:---:|:---:|:---:|
| 1 | 1 | Near Past | -2 | Urgent | +1 |
| 2 | 1 | Distant Past | -3 | Patient | -1 |
| 3 | 1 | Near Future | +2 | Urgent | +1 |
| 4 | 1 | Present | 0 | Patient | -1 |
| 5 | 1 | Immediate Past | -1 | Patient | -1 |
| 6 | 1 | Distant Future | +3 | Urgent | +1 |
| 7 | 1 | Immediate Future | +1 | Urgent | +1 |
| 8 | 1 | Present | 0 | Urgent | +1 |
| 9 | 1 | Immediate Future | +1 | Patient | -1 |
| | **Total** | | **Total** | | **Total** |
| Members | 9 | Future | +1 | Urgency | +1 |

As you use these tools to diagnose your own teams, you will see that results can vary dramatically. Let's examine some teams I have encountered and score them using these tools. We can relate the analysis to actual issues that arose during the project and learn how the team adjusted to keep the team wheel rolling along.

# All Talk, No Action

The team shown in Table 8.4 had thirteen members. The balanced team would have one or two team members at each step; on this team, Types 1 and 6 were overrepresented, and Type 8 was missing. As this team moved through the steps in problem solving, there was a constant tendency to revert back to Step 1 to reexamine the problems. This tendency was especially strong in Steps 2, 3, and 4.

As a result of the predominance of Type 6 members, this team also wanted to minimize Step 5 activities (logical analysis) and move quickly into Step 6 (planning). Since there was less representation of Type 7 energy than Type 6, the team had trouble moving into Step 7 to promote the team's plan to stakeholders.

With no Type 8 representation on the team, no one was strongly advocating the need to start acting on the plan. As such, the team stalled and would even get pulled back to Step 1 as new problems arose. A team that is out of balance in this way can have a tendency to go around and around without ever moving into Step 8, the action-oriented Implementation phase in which the team actually solves the original problem. I call this team "All Talk, No Action."

## Table 8.4 – Type Distribution of All Talk, No Action Team

| Enneagram Type | No. of Team Members | Wheel Inflation |
|:---:|:---:|:---:|
| 1 | 3 | Overinflated |
| 2 | 1 | OK |
| 3 | 1 | OK |
| 4 | 1 | OK |
| 5 | 1 | OK |
| 6 | 3 | Overinflated |
| 7 | 2 | OK |
| 8 | 0 | Flat |
| 9 | 1 | OK |
| **Total** | | |
| Members | 13 | |

Table 8.5 shows the results of the time analysis of the All Talk, No Action team. This team has a strong (+4) inclination towards the future, driven by the concentration of Type 6 team members. For balance, a team of this size would have a future inclination of +1 to +2. At +4, a team may have trouble bringing itself back into the present to work on solving the problem. And indeed, that is exactly what I saw in this case.

In terms of the team's sense of urgency, it scores +5. Ideally a team of this size will have a score of +1 to +2. At +5, frenetic energy will translate to debate, arguments, and more planning. In other words, there will be a whole lot of talking and not a lot of action.

## Table 8.5 – Time Analysis of All Talk, No Action Team

| Enneagram Type | No. of Team Members | Mental Energy Timeline | Timeline Weighting | Sense of Urgency/ Patience | Urgency/ Patience Weighting |
|---|---|---|---|---|---|
| 1 | 3 | Near Past (-2) | -6 | Urgent (+1) | +3 |
| 2 | 1 | Distant Past (-3) | -3 | Patient (-1) | -1 |
| 3 | 1 | Near Future (+2) | +2 | Urgent (+1) | +1 |
| 4 | 1 | Present (0) | 0 | Patient (-1) | -1 |
| 5 | 1 | Immediate Past (-1) | -1 | Patient (-1) | -1 |
| 6 | 3 | Distant Future (+3) | +9 | Urgent (+1) | +3 |
| 7 | 2 | Immediate Future (+1) | +2 | Urgent (+1) | +2 |
| 8 | 0 | Present (0) | 0 | Urgent (+1) | 0 |
| 9 | 1 | Immediate Future (+1) | +1 | Patient (-1) | -1 |
| **Total** | | | **Total** | | **Total** |
| Members | 13 | Future | +4 | Urgent | +5 |

Table 8.6 shows the brain dominances of this All Talk, No Action team. There is a high concentration of right-PFC types from the 1s and the 6s and a high concentration of left amygdala types from the Head-Thinking-Anxiety center. The combination of right PFC dominance and left amygdala dominance corresponds to Type 6; thus, these concentrations will give this team an overall style of Type 6, with a proclivity to overemphasize Step 6 (planning) and not move to Step 7 (promoting).

## Table 8.6 – Brain Dominance Analysis of All Talk, No Action Team

| Enneagram Type | No. of Team Members | PFC Dominance | PFC Weighting | Amygdala Dominance | Amygdala Weighting |
|---|---|---|---|---|---|
| 1 | 3 | Pessimistic | +3 | Fear unaware | +3 |
| 2 | 1 | Pessimistic | +1 | Dual | +1 |
| 3 | 1 | Optimistic | +1 | Dual | +1 |
| 4 | 1 | Dual | +1 | Dual | +1 |
| 5 | 1 | Dual | +1 | Fear aware | +1 |
| 6 | 3 | Pessimistic | +3 | Fear aware | +3 |
| 7 | 2 | Optimistic | +2 | Fear aware | +2 |
| 8 | 0 | Optimistic | 0 | Fear unaware | 0 |
| 9 | 1 | Dual | +1 | Fear unaware | +1 |
| | **Total** | | **Total** | | **Total** |
| Members | 13 | Pessimistic | +7 | Fear unaware | +4 |
| | | Optimistic | +3 | Fear aware | +6 |
| | | Dual | +3 | Dual | +3 |

Armed with information about your team members and analysis of their dynamics, you will be better prepared to overcome some of the tendencies inherent in the specific team composition. You will need to slow down some teams to keep them from rushing frenetically from step to step. At times, you will need to pull the team into the present to keep them from focusing too far into the future or the past. And you will need to encourage your team to get out of its "box"—in this case, by presenting a plan to the broader set of stakeholders and getting started on implementation.

If you had leeway to adjust the composition of an All Talk, No Action team such as this, then you would want to consider reducing the number of 1s and 6s on the team and, in their place, add a Type 8 and a Type 5. As shown in Table 8.7, these adjustments would give the team complete representation of all types and energies, with a +2 score for future perspective and a +3 score for sense of urgency. This team would be much more balanced and avoid most of the pitfalls of the original All Talk, No Action team.

**Table 8.7 – Time Analysis of Adjusted All Talk, No Action Team**

| Enneagram Type | No. of Team Members | Mental Energy Timeline | Timeline Weighting | Sense of Urgency/ Patience | Urgency/ Patience Weighting |
|---|---|---|---|---|---|
| 1 | 2 | Near Past (-2) | -4 | Urgent (+1) | +2 |
| 2 | 1 | Distant Past (-3) | -3 | Patient (-1) | -1 |
| 3 | 1 | Near Future (+2) | +2 | Urgent (+1) | +1 |
| 4 | 1 | Present (0) | 0 | Patient (-1) | -1 |
| 5 | 2 | Immediate Past (-1) | -2 | Patient (-1) | -2 |
| 6 | 2 | Distant Future (+3) | +6 | Urgent (+1) | +2 |
| 7 | 2 | Immediate Future (+1) | +2 | Urgent (+1) | +2 |
| 8 | 1 | Present (0) | 0 | Urgent (+1) | +1 |
| 9 | 1 | Immediate Future (+1) | +1 | Patient (-1) | -1 |
| **Total** | | | **Total** | | **Total** |
| Members | 13 | Future | +2 | Urgent | +3 |

You can see that, depending on your team makeup, there can be any number of bumps, dips, and flats as you move through the problem-solving process. It is important as the facilitator of the process to understand the team makeup, anticipate the trouble spots, and enable the team to compensate for concentrations and deficiencies in leadership in any one step. Let's take a look at another common example.

# Paralysis by Analysis

As I work with teams and see how the strengths and weaknesses influence progress, I realize that there are many well-worn clichés that describe these challenges. Let's examine another team that I commonly find in technology companies: Paralysis by Analysis.

Table 8.8 shows that this particular team has a concentration of Type 5 team members and a deficiency of Type 6 members, making the team wheel overinflated in Step 5 (logical analysis) and flat (no representation) in Step 6 (planning). This team also has no representation in Type 4, so there would be a tendency to discount negative emotional reactions to ideas and keep open more options than necessary and moving into Step 5; this tendency would bog down the team that much more.

The Paralysis by Analysis team will play to their strength—analyzing the problem and brainstorming solutions—and will be content to do so without feeling compelled to decide what to do with the results of the analysis. There will also be a pullback to rehashing the problem due to the overrepresentation of Type 1s on this particular team—a tendency that Type 5s would not resist.

**Table 8.8 – Type Distribution of Paralysis by Analysis Team**

| Enneagram Type | No. of Team Members | Wheel Inflation |
|:---:|:---:|:---:|
| 1 | 3 | Overinflated |
| 2 | 1 | OK |
| 3 | 2 | OK |
| 4 | 0 | Flat |
| 5 | 3 | Overinflated |
| 6 | 0 | Flat |
| 7 | 1 | OK |
| 8 | 1 | OK |
| 9 | 1 | OK |

| Total | |
|:---:|:---:|
| Members | 12 |

Because of the overinflation of Type 5 and the flat in Type 6, this team will have a particularly difficult challenge moving from Step 5 to Step 6. In general, any team will face a challenge moving to the next step when the type corresponding to the current step is overrepresented and the subsequent step's dynamic is not represented. This example is particularly acute.

Analyzing the brain dominances of the Paralysis by Analysis team (Table 8.9), we find that this team is well balanced. PFC dominances are balanced between right, left, and dual, with four each on the team. Amygdala balance is not bad, with a slight overrepresentation of right amygdala and underrepresentation of dual. The brain dominances in and of themselves do not reveal a picture of a team that is off balance, like the type concentration (wheel) analysis predicts. What else may be going on?

### Table 8.9 – Brain Dominance Analysis
### of Paralysis by Analysis Team

| Enneagram Type | No. of Team Members | PFC Dominance | PFC Weighting | Amygdala Dominance | Amygdala Weighting |
|---|---|---|---|---|---|
| 1 | 3 | Pessimistic | +3 | Fear unaware | +3 |
| 2 | 1 | Pessimistic | +1 | Dual | +1 |
| 3 | 2 | Optimistic | +2 | Dual | +2 |
| 4 | 0 | Dual | 0 | Dual | 0 |
| 5 | 3 | Dual | +3 | Fear aware | +3 |
| 6 | 0 | Pessimistic | 0 | Fear aware | 0 |
| 7 | 1 | Optimistic | +1 | Fear aware | +1 |
| 8 | 1 | Optimistic | +1 | Fear unaware | +1 |
| 9 | 1 | Dual | +1 | Fear unaware | +1 |
| | **Total** | | **Total** | | **Total** |
| Members | 12 | Pessimistic | +4 | Fear unaware | +5 |
| | | Optimistic | +4 | Fear aware | +4 |
| | | Dual | +4 | Dual | +3 |

Turning to the time analysis in Table 8.10, we discover a team that is highly focused on the past with a -6 score. Ideally, a team this size would be a +1 to +2, so this team is strongly anchored in the past. On the other hand, the team urgency score of +2 is just right for this team. The challenge for this team's project facilitator will be to keep the vision of the future always in the team's sights. Otherwise, they will continue to discuss the problem and analyze solutions without ever moving forward to attain the goal.

## Table 8.10 – Time Analysis of Paralysis by Analysis Team

| Enneagram Type | No. of Team Members | Mental Energy Timeline | Timeline Weighting | Sense of Urgency/ Patience | Urgency/ Patience Weighting |
|---|---|---|---|---|---|
| 1 | 3 | Near Past (-2) | -6 | Urgent (+1) | +3 |
| 2 | 1 | Distant Past (-3) | -3 | Patient (-1) | -1 |
| 3 | 2 | Near Future (+2) | +4 | Urgent (+1) | +2 |
| 4 | 0 | Present (0) | 0 | Patient (-1) | 0 |
| 5 | 3 | Immediate Past (-1) | -3 | Patient (-1) | -3 |
| 6 | 0 | Distant Future (+3) | 0 | Urgent (+1) | 0 |
| 7 | 1 | Immediate Future (+1) | +1 | Urgent (+1) | +1 |
| 8 | 1 | Present (0) | 0 | Urgent (+1) | +1 |
| 9 | 1 | Immediate Future (+1) | +1 | Patient (-1) | -1 |
| | **Total** | | **Total** | | **Total** |
| Members | 12 | Past | -6 | Urgent | +2 |

Have you ever encountered a team that is paralyzed in a state of analysis? In this case, even the Type 8 team member who would normally compel the team to action was insecure enough to move along their path of disintegration towards the behaviors of the observing Type 5. In this state, they could not compel the stuck team to move forward.

This Paralysis by Analysis team needs a good dose of Type 6 energy—energy that will find a path through the analysis to create Plans A and B for the team. Also, the team needs the anxious energy— the threat of consequences of *not* deciding and *not* moving forward towards a solution—to break out of its paralysis. If the team lacks that energy, then the designated facilitator needs to understand this deficiency and supplement the team with the energy it needs.

In practice, I find that placing time limits on Step 5 (and on every step for that matter) helps keep the team motivated to complete the work and move on to the next step. Knowing that the team is going to move on after a certain point, one way or another, can motivate team members to complete the analysis necessary to make a decision.

Also, Type 5 energy is not particularly adept at prioritizing which ideas to analyze over others, especially if there is a "flat" in Type 4 energy. The brain dominance analysis of this particular team shows that they have the capacity to make an informed decision about the direction to proceed. Since the Type 2 team member has access to the Type 4 dynamic along their path of integration, enlisting the 2 to help cull emotionally unattractive ideas would be a useful approach to narrow the scope of work in Step 5.

If there is latitude to make adjustments to team composition, then reducing the concentration of Type 1s and Type 5s by one member each and adding two Type 6 members modify the Mental Energy Timeline score to a reasonable +3 from the previous -6. This shift in perspective will sway the team to a future-looking orientation while maintaining a balance of brain dominances. The urgency level will increase from +2 to +4, so the tendency to rush ahead may become a new challenge, which would need to be monitored.

# Fail Fast

One problem-solving team pathology has become so common it is now considered a "feature," especially in Silicon Valley. Fail Fast is the approach to try different things quickly until you hit on an idea that works. Other sayings that come to mind for Fail Fast are "Ready, fire, aim" and "If at first you don't succeed, try, try again."

Imagine that you have a problem in Step 1 but then skip Step 2 (in which you engage all stakeholders and build a team representing strengths in all the steps of problem solving). Instead you jump to Step

3 and generate an idea to solve the problem that you feel may work (Step 4). Then, you minimize the analytical (Step 5), planning (Step 6), and promoting (Step 7) activities and jump straight to implementing the solution (Step 8). The idea will likely turn out to be an inadequate long-term solution even if it does work in the short term. When the inadequacy becomes apparent and intolerable, the team moves back to Step 1 and Fail Fast repeats. Table 8.11 illustrates a team that embraced this approach.

### Table 8.11 – Type Distribution of Fail Fast Team

| Enneagram Type | No. of Team Members | Wheel Inflation |
|---|---|---|
| 1 | 1 | OK |
| 2 | 1 | OK |
| 3 | 0 | Flat |
| 4 | 1 | OK |
| 5 | 1 | OK |
| 6 | 0 | Flat |
| 7 | 1 | OK |
| 8 | 1 | OK |
| 9 | 0 | Flat |

| Total | |
|---|---|
| Members | 6 |

This Fail Fast team was overwhelmed by action-oriented Type 8 energy. In this case, the overrepresentation of the 8 dynamic was not from multiple Type 8 team members but from the culture of the organization and the Type 8's strong personality. Type 8 tends to attract Types 2 and 5 team members, so they are represented on this team along with the 1, 4, and 7, but they all tend to become submissive in the presence of a dominant Type 8.

**Table 8.12 – Brain Dominance Analysis of Fail Fast Team**

| Enneagram Type | No. of Team Members | PFC Dominance | PFC Weighting | Amygdala Dominance | Amygdala Weighting |
|---|---|---|---|---|---|
| 1 | 1 | Pessimistic | +1 | Fear unaware | +1 |
| 2 | 1 | Pessimistic | +1 | Dual | +1 |
| 3 | 0 | Optimistic | 0 | Dual | 0 |
| 4 | 1 | Dual | +1 | Dual | +1 |
| 5 | 1 | Dual | +1 | Fear aware | +1 |
| 6 | 0 | Pessimistic | 0 | Fear aware | 0 |
| 7 | 1 | Optimistic | +1 | Fear aware | +1 |
| 8 | 1 | Optimistic | +1 | Fear unaware | +1 |
| 9 | 0 | Dual | 0 | Fear unaware | 0 |

| | **Total** | | **Total** | | **Total** |
|---|---|---|---|---|---|
| Members | 6 | Pessimistic | +2 | Fear unaware | +2 |
| | | Optimistic | +2 | Fear aware | +2 |
| | | Dual | +2 | Dual | +2 |

Referring to Table 8.12, this six-member team does have balanced brain dominances. Often I find that team members coalesce in a way that provides brain dominance balance, and this team was a great example of that tendency.

## Table 8.13 – Time Analysis of Fail Fast Team

| Enneagram Type | No. of Team Members | Mental Energy Timeline | Timeline Weighting | Sense of Urgency/ Patience | Urgency/ Patience Weighting |
|---|---|---|---|---|---|
| 1 | 1 | Near Past (-2) | -2 | Urgent (+1) | +1 |
| 2 | 1 | Distant Past (-3) | -3 | Patient (-1) | -1 |
| 3 | 0 | Near Future (+2) | 0 | Urgent (+1) | 0 |
| 4 | 1 | Present (0) | 0 | Patient (-1) | -1 |
| 5 | 1 | Immediate Past (-1) | -1 | Patient (-1) | -1 |
| 6 | 0 | Distant Future (+3) | 0 | Urgent (+1) | 0 |
| 7 | 1 | Immediate Future (+1) | +1 | Urgent (+1) | +1 |
| 8 | 1 | Present (0) | 0 | Urgent (+1) | +1 |
| 9 | 0 | Immediate Future (+1) | 0 | Patient (-1) | 0 |

| | **Total** | | **Total** | | **Total** |
|---|---|---|---|---|---|
| Members | 6 | Past | -5 | Neutral | 0 |

Table 8.13 shows that this Fail Fast team was anchored in the past. While the past orientation does not prevent the team from jumping into action to try to solve the problem (due to the dominant, action-oriented Type 8), it does prevent the team from thinking through the ramifications and consequences of the proposed solution, which makes the outcome uncertain. Curiously, the team urgency is scored as 0 or neutral. From my perspective as a Type 6, it seemed as if this team had no urgency to actually solve the problem, in spite of the urgency to act under the influence of the dominant Type 8 leader.

The Fail Fast method of problem solving has become popular in the software development world where trying and scrapping code can be less expensive than developing a robust solution the first time around. When the cost of failure is low, Fail Fast is a rational approach. On the other hand, as the cost of failure increases, the effectiveness of this approach goes down, and proceeding methodically through all the steps in the problem-solving process becomes more important.

I often see the Fail Fast approach used in organizations with a strong Type 8 leader who does not suffer a lot of discussion and wants the team in the action-oriented Step 8. Generally, Type 8s are not afraid of failure—or even of being wrong. Once they appreciate that the team is moving in the wrong direction, the 8 leader can quickly correct course and move the team in a new, more promising direction.

## The Strong Boss

One of my clients is a strong Type 8 leader. He is a strategic thinker and as smart as they come. He guides himself and his team to deliver consistently great results. Yet, he complains to me that his team fails to think for themselves, so he feels the need to maintain a hands-on approach and monitor the team continually. He finds this tiring and aggravating and wishes he could be a better delegator. What is happening here?

As I interacted with my client's team, I discovered that they were very reactive. They understood that he valued action highly; therefore, they took direction from the boss and turned that into action as quickly as possible. There was little need to highlight problems to the boss since the boss set the agenda on the important problems to address. They also minimized analysis and planning activities since these activities took time and stood in the way of starting to act.

The boss's leadership style created an action-oriented culture, reflecting the Implementation step in problem solving (Step 8). The team members attracted to this organization respond well to that leadership style. Once the boss set the direction, the team found little need for further conversation about the problem (Step 1). By moving directly to Step 2, people would organize and figure out how they would respond to the boss's direction. Ideas would be generated (Step 3), but the team would find there was little value in reacting to or analyzing the ideas (Steps 4/5) and building plans (Step 6) around them. They would present a promising idea (Step 7) to the boss for review and approval, and the boss—being the smart, strategic person he is—would quickly assess the idea and either approve it, modify it, or send the team back to the drawing board. Essentially, the team would take shortcuts in order to move as quickly as possible to the Implementation phase (Step 8).

This action-oriented problem-solving style produces results quickly, whether good or bad. You could characterize this as an iterative method. Because the boss was experienced, there was a high probability that the ideas he directed the team to pursue would be successful. The cost of this approach was that he had to spend a tremendous amount of energy setting the direction, reviewing ideas, and monitoring results.

In working with this team, I found that I had to start at the end with the neglected Integration step (Step 9). I reviewed with the team how they solved problems, and we determined what was working well and what was not. Out of this discussion came a list of potential problems (Step 1) that the team considered important to address. Reviewing this list with the boss, we quickly agreed on the important problems. The big difference was that the problems were the team's problems, not the boss's. Now the team was highly motivated to solve these problems.

I had the team spend more time analyzing different ideas for solutions and putting together a well-thought-out plan before presenting the plan to the boss. The team put together a terrific proposal of which they were genuinely proud. The boss was equally pleased and gave them permission to proceed, which the team did with considerable enthusiasm.

The Type 8 boss learned how his personal leadership style was affecting the team's performance. The problems he experienced with his team were the result of his own behavior as much as his team's. When he allowed them some say in choosing the problems to solve, the team delivered great results and took far less oversight, which made the boss happy.

---

There are many clichés for teams that struggle such as "half-baked idea," "heart in the right place," and "look before you leap." You can now imagine the teams and compositions of Enneagram types that would result in these descriptions. The next team I will describe is one I dubbed "Under the Rug."

# Under the Rug

The Under the Rug team (Table 8.14) was a smaller team of six members. Like a family, they were thrust together not by choice but by circumstance, and all of them had already worked together for a long time. Type 2 energy was overrepresented, and the team was bereft of any representation of the Gut-Intuitive-Anger center. Without the Type 1 dynamic, problems remained unaired and problematic situations languished. I find that families will similarly avoid discussing difficult problems and often go as far as to hide problems by "sweeping them under the rug."

## Table 8.14 – Type Distribution of Under the Rug Team

| Enneagram Type | No. of Team Members | Wheel Inflation |
|:---:|:---:|:---:|
| 1 | 0 | Flat |
| 2 | 2 | Overinflated |
| 3 | 1 | OK |
| 4 | 1 | OK |
| 5 | 1 | OK |
| 6 | 1 | OK |
| 7 | 0 | Flat |
| 8 | 0 | Flat |
| 9 | 0 | Flat |

| | **Total** | |
|:---:|:---:|:---:|
| Members | 6 | |

Curiously, when I worked with this team and brought problems to light, the team engaged and was eager to take on the problems. The concentration of Type 2 energy came through with enthusiasm to help solve the problems. The abrupt transition from completely ignoring problems to eagerly wanting to solve them showed the importance of having a Type 1 voice in the mix to ensure that problems are identified and communicated.

As we worked through the problem-solving process and arrived at a plan to implement solutions, the effort stalled. There was no Type 7 energy to promote the plan to all the stakeholders who would be affected. Thankfully, the 2s stepped up at this point to pull the effort through. Having developed a sound plan in Step 6, they understood how to get everyone needed on board and how to get the implementation rolling. I was impressed by the flexibility and willingness of the 2s to assume additional roles and duties when the group needed it.

From a brain dominance point of view (Table 8.15), the PFC had balanced representation but the amygdala did not—the Gut-Intuitive-Anger center wasn't represented on the team. In this case, the dual-dominance types, especially Type 2s, were able to step into the role of the right amygdala types, the Gut-Intuitive-Anger types, when the team needed them.

## Table 8.15 – Brain Dominance Analysis of Under the Rug Team

| Enneagram Type | No. of Team Members | PFC Dominance | PFC Weighting | Amygdala Dominance | Amygdala Weighting |
|---|---|---|---|---|---|
| 1 | 0 | Pessimistic | 0 | Fear unaware | 0 |
| 2 | 2 | Pessimistic | +2 | Dual | +2 |
| 3 | 1 | Optimistic | +1 | Dual | +1 |
| 4 | 1 | Dual | +1 | Dual | +1 |
| 5 | 1 | Dual | +1 | Fear aware | +1 |
| 6 | 1 | Pessimistic | +1 | Fear aware | +1 |
| 7 | 0 | Optimistic | 0 | Fear aware | 0 |
| 8 | 0 | Optimistic | 0 | Fear unaware | 0 |
| 9 | 0 | Dual | 0 | Fear unaware | 0 |
| | **Total** | | **Total** | | **Total** |
| Members | 6 | Pessimistic | +3 | Fear unaware | 0 |
| | | Optimistic | +1 | Fear aware | +2 |
| | | Dual | +2 | Dual | +4 |

The Mental Energy Timeline analysis shown in Table 8.16 is particularly illustrative of this team's propensity to sweep problems under the rug. For a team of six members, you would want to see a Mental Energy Timeline score of +1. In this case, the timeline score was -2, driven by the concentration of Type 2 energy. Without the inclination to think about the future, it is easy to see why there would be no vision for a beautiful world without problems. For team urgency, ideally you would want to see a score of +1. In this case, the team urgency score was -2, so there was no strong motivation to uncover and solve problems. For these reasons, the problems languished under the rug.

### Table 8.16 – Time Analysis of the Under the Rug Team

| Enneagram Type | No. of Team Members | Mental Energy Timeline | Timeline Weighting | Sense of Urgency/ Patience | Urgency/ Patience Weighting |
|---|---|---|---|---|---|
| 1 | 0 | Near Past (-2) | 0 | Urgent (+1) | 0 |
| 2 | 2 | Distant Past (-3) | -6 | Patient (-1) | -2 |
| 3 | 1 | Near Future (+2) | 2 | Urgent (+1) | 1 |
| 4 | 1 | Present (0) | 0 | Patient (-1) | -1 |
| 5 | 1 | Immediate Past (-1) | -1 | Patient (-1) | -1 |
| 6 | 1 | Distant Future (+3) | 3 | Urgent (+1) | 1 |
| 7 | 0 | Immediate Future (+1) | 0 | Urgent (+1) | 0 |
| 8 | 0 | Present (0) | 0 | Urgent (+1) | 0 |
| 9 | 0 | Immediate Future (+1) | 0 | Patient (-1) | 0 |
| | **Total** | | **Total** | | **Total** |
| | 6 | Past | -2 | Patient | -2 |

For this particular team composition, the only additional ingredient necessary to compel this team to action was my participation as facilitator. The most valuable contribution I made was to have the team thoroughly describe the problem and create a vision for the future. In other words, I was able to supplement the team's lack of Type 1 energy at the beginning of the process. Because of the concentration of Type 2 energy, there was a smooth handoff to the next step in the process, and the momentum grew from there.

Realizing the lack of representation of Type 7 and Type 8 energy on the team, I worked with one of the Type 2 members and coached them to fill those roles as needed. Being a Type 2, they were more than happy to help!

If one of the Type 2 members had been unable or unwilling to step into the leadership role for Steps 7 and 8, then the addition of a Type 7 and a Type 8 to the team would have been helpful. Not only would these types fix the flats in the team wheel, both of these types bring a sense of urgency to the team, and both tend to be future oriented, which could balance out the time elements of this team.

## Summary

When described in theory, problem solving can seem easy and straightforward. In practice, it may not be as smooth. When we examine the composition and dynamics of our team, we can anticipate likely bumps and dips in the problem-solving process. The tools described here enable you to understand your team and its inclinations. By finding the overinflated, underinflated, and flat spots on the team wheel, you can predict how smooth your ride through the problem-solving steps will be. The balance of brain dominances will give you an indication of how well the team will work together. The analysis of time sensibility—both Mental Energy Timeline and urgency—will give you a sense of the team's natural inclinations to get to the goal.

While you may not be able to avoid imbalances in your team, you can use these tools to facilitate your team and guide it through the bumpy spots in problem solving.

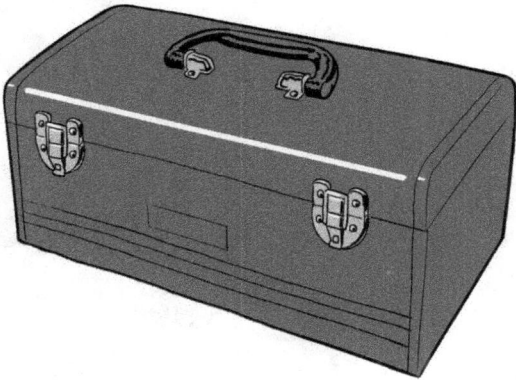

# CHAPTER 9

# The Meaning of Life

I f you are like me, there are points in your life at which you asked questions like, "Why am I here? What is the purpose of life? What is the purpose of *my* life?"

I think the Enneagram gives us an interesting framework to investigate these questions. According to theory, early in life each of us acquires a lifelong predisposition to assume one of the Enneagram types based on our brain dominances. Those dominances imbue us with talents that allow us to contribute to the rest of our group, our family, our community, our organization, our country, our world. And those talents complement everyone else's talents and are crucial to specific roles in problem solving.

This framing has allowed me to completely accept myself and how I am in all my 6-ness. It has allowed me to explore how I can use my Type 6 gifts to their full potential and contribute to the success of all the groups in which I participate. Indeed, I feel that my gifts give me purpose and show me the way to contribute fully in life. I think the Enneagram can show the way to a purposeful life for all types.

Furthermore, the Enneagram provides a framework to understand and appreciate the dynamics and contributions of every Enneagram type. No one type is better or worse than any other. Each type plays a crucial role in the success and progress of the entire group. I appreciate how the problem-solving process provides a way to understand the *hows* and *whens* of each type's contribution.

Sometimes we may feel underappreciated for the specific contributions that our innate type offers. That too can be understood in the context of problem solving. There is a time and place for each dynamic. If your group is not at a point in time that requires the contribution represented by your Enneagram type, you may struggle. Do not despair; the cycle continues and your time will come again. I have learned that it is best at times to suppress my 6-ness—sometimes it is neither appreciated nor relevant. Yet, as sure as the sun rises, there will be a periodic need for the 6 perspective.

The Enneagram also shows us how to access other dynamics, particularly along our path of integration, which enable us to contribute generously at multiple steps in the problem-solving process. As we transcend our innate type, our perspective broadens and allows us to see more and contribute in meaningful ways at all steps in problem solving.

People connected to a community that perennially devalues their innate type may find themselves feeling out of place. For instance, imagine an organization tuned to perfectionism and predominantly operating in the Type 1 dynamic. While Type 1s would thrive, Type 8s would be continually frustrated. Understanding both yourself and your associations will help clarify why you are frustrated and provide a path to finding communities that more highly value your particular contributions.

While some groups do require specialization in specific dynamics—firefighters (Type 8), surgeons (Type 1), etc.—any group would benefit from the perspectives of all Enneagram types. Every community will be continuously cycling around the problem-solving wheel, and the more the nine perspectives are represented, the smoother the ride will be.

Enneagram dynamics are built into humanity. They emerge naturally from our respective brain dominances. One way or another, humans progress through the problem-solving process, whether smoothly or bumpily. We may take three steps forward and two steps back at times, but we do inevitably keep moving forward. The problem with the ad hoc approach is that it takes a lot longer to get to the goal. Sometimes you do not have time for progress to occur naturally. Sometimes you need to accelerate in order to meet a deadline.

When pressed for time, an organized, systematic approach will help you progress smoothly through the problem-solving process. This is especially true when the stakes are high. The Enneagram-based problem-solving approach will help you and your team reach your goals and realize success.

On a global scale, humanity faces ever bigger challenges. Some are natural and some we created. Our perennial problem of access to fresh water and nutritious food is now intensified by climate change. Climate change poses an existential threat to humanity, with a looming deadline to which we are seemingly insensitive. By the time we do register the threat and decide to take action, I hope it is not too late. I sincerely believe that the Enneagram problem-solving process will help humanity rally around practical solutions and implement them speedily.

Those were some heavy Type 6 thoughts, so allow me to end on a happier note. More and more research highlights the human need for personal development. For instance, there is a research paper that highlights how people who pursue personal growth and interactions with others in their leisure time are happier than others.[1] This is not

---

1  Andreja Brajša-Žganec, Marina Merkaš, and Iva Šverko, "Quality of Life and Leisure Activities: How Do Leisure Activities Contribute to Subjective Well-Being?" *Social Indicators Research 102*, no. 1 (May 2011): 81–91. doi.org/10.1007/s11205-010-9724-2.

unique to any one country or culture as this study was conducted in thirty-three different countries!

In this book, I have shared tools for strengthening your personal relationships and developing your innate talents. My hope is that you will make the most of your gifts and relationships by contributing to and cooperating with others—if for no other reason than to pursue your own happiness.